Turning the Pages
(Seeking Clarity)

By Bro. James Earl Smith

Turning The Pages

Copyright, 2017 by James Earl Smith

ISBN-13: 978-1-944583-18-7

This book is published by Laurel Rose Publishing, 1930 Holston Rd, Como, MS 38619

TEL: 662-501-7129
E-MAIL: laurelrosepublishing@gmail.com
WEBSITE: www.laurelrosepublishing.com

Printed in the UNITED STATES OF AMERICA

Turning the pages
(Seeking clarity)

Turning the pages is a selection of common asked questions among church goers. The questions are frequently asked but rarely considered essential for building the Christian character by some leaders. However, the answer to these questions should make an impact in the mind of every Christian believer. As you turn the pages of this book, it is my hope that you gain a deeper insight into keeping and understanding God word to its fullest. In the words of our Savior "ask and it shall be given; seek and ye shall find; knock at the door and it shall be opened." A closed mouth cannot be heard; an absent traveler cannot be seen: an empty mind can serve no purpose nor can a shut book reveal knowledge. If ever we want to learn, be heard or seen, the first steps and efforts must be made by us. Salvation is free but we must learn what to do in order to take advantage of it.

Acknowledgement

First I would like to thank and acknowledge God for the gift of the Holy Spirit that has given me the insight to write this book. In a time when people are turning away from the commandments of God to seek their own personal desires, it is important that they not forget that for all their deeds God will bring them into judgment. Mankind cannot do what they want to in life and not expect repercussions. I acknowledge and commend all those who continue to teach and preach the true word and gospel of Jesus Christ knowing that the end draws nigh. I acknowledge that the scriptures are being fulfilled before our eyes each and every day but the lust and desires of the flesh have blinded many to the truths of God. As it is every born again Christian duty to lead others to Christ using the gift(s) that God has given unto them, I take pleasure in using the gift of my literary and spiritual knowledge to influence others in every way I can. Whether through teaching, writing, helps, speaking, praying, comforting, or whatever the means, I take pleasure in doing and promoting all that is just. According to scripture, the best thing that a man can achieve in life above all other things is a good name. Such an accomplishment does not come easily but it is achievable with the help of God and one' determination to do the things that are right and honest in the sight of God and men alike. I acknowledge this day and every day that the living God is still on the throne and watches and cares for the well beings of his children needs both day and night. I further acknowledge through experience that God is a promise keeping God that always keeps his words to those who shows their love for him by keeping his commandments.

Preface

In this age of confusion overbearing with technology and deceitfulness, men everywhere are seeking answers to solving their personal and Nations' problems. What many fail to realize is that the answer to today' problems can only be found in God. Satan has deceived a vast majority of the world people into thinking that man has the solution to fixing our world problems. The origin of the problem began in the Garden of Eden with the first man and woman breaking of the commandment of God for pleasures of the eyes and heart. There's a song that church choirs often sing that points out the fact that whatever we need, we can find it in the word of God. They sing the song but many fail to realize the lyric to the song is true.

From a mother's womb
Shapen in iniquity
Destiny is born

In the book of Hosea, we read where God says my people perish for the lack of knowledge. If we would be true to ourselves today, we'd realize that many people lack the knowledge of God in their lives. They have their fancy bibles and mechanical toys but rarely ever read or follow the written words. Ecclesiastes 3:15 says, *"That which hath been is now; and that which is to be hath already been; and God requireth that which is past."* *"There is no new **thing** under the sun Ecclesiastes 1:9a".* Sin is as much alive today as it was in times past. People today are committing the same sins their forefathers committed. As he required men of the past to repent and turn back to him to receive the healing of their lands and nations, God requires the same of us today.

> What we sow; we reap
> Man's actions bow in return
> Blessings or cursing

In the first world, the wickedness of man was so great and God saw that every imagination of his heart was only evil continually. Because of man' continuous pursuit of evil, God destroyed the first world but gave mankind another chance through Noah and his family. Mankind seems to be growing toward that trend once again. With every type of crime known to man on the rise, many are afraid to go out of their doors. Though evil is growing worse and worse, instead of increasing, church memberships everywhere are decreasing in numbers. Instead of people turning to God for the answer, people are turning to guns and other means of protection for comfort. God is the author of peace and prosperity and only he can restore peace back to our lands and nations. In the world, as a People, we often place our trust in candidates for leadership that make unusual promises that even they themselves know they cannot keep but our spiritual leader, Christ, is the king of peace and a promise keeper who has not broken a promise yet. Though the best of men may try their best to solve their nation's problems, each and every one of them will fail.

We as a world of people are divided in our views of what is right and what is wrong. Jealousy, hatred, envy, family ties, friendships and the likes, often cloud our decisions. People are more concerned about what they want out of life, impressing others, or hurting others feelings, than what God says is best for them. In the heart of many, the love of God has grown cold and the love for the ways of the world is growing stronger. Even church going people, who know what is right, are ignoring God' words to follow their own desires. They fail to reflect back on what happen to Eve because of her desire for what the fruit of the forbidden tree had to offer. Man' dreams, ways, desires, and even his life, will someday pass away but God' words will never pass away. God has laid out the plan of salvation and the order in which men are to live in this life; if we desire blessings and prosperity in this life and eternal life in the world to come, we must follow God' order and plan. There is no other way of securing our success in this world and the world to come other than what God has already put in place.

In Isaiah 55: 8-11, we read. *"For my thoughts **are** not your thoughts, nor **are** your ways My ways," says the Lord. "For **as** the heavens are higher than the earth, so are My ways higher than your ways, and My thoughts than your thoughts. For as the rain comes down, and the snow from heaven, and do not return there, but water the earth, and makes it bring forth and bud, that it may give seed to the sower and bread to the eater. So shall My word be that goes forth from My mouth; it shall not return to Me void, but it shall accomplish what I please, and it shall prosper **in the thing** for which I sent it.* In the book of Luke 21:33, we see where the Lord says, *"Heaven and earth will pass away, but My words will by no means pass away."*

Deeds done in darkness
Bear sins eager to be known
Light will reclaim them

How long will we, as the people of God, continue to allow the deceiving methods of Satan to stir us in the wrong way? From the beginning, Satan used his tactics to deceive Eve in believing that God is not true to his word. **(I say Eve because the scripture clearly states that Adam was not deceived 2 Timothy 2:14; however Adam did sin by eating the fruit also; therefore, he too was guilty of breaking God commandment and \like Eve, gave up his and all his descendants chance to live forever without dying a physical death. Because of God love for his creation, after Adam and Eve' sin, God prophesied that he would send a Savior into the world that would intervene between the woman' seed and the serpent' (the devil') seed Genesis (3:15).** In Genesis the third chapter, we see where Eve testified that God had said that if they ate of the forbidden fruit they would surely die but the devil through the voice of the serpent said "ye shall not surely die". Here we see the first recorded deceiving lie of Satan. Listening to this lie cost the first man and woman eternal life. **(Keep in mind God said to Adam; of the tree of the knowledge of good and evil, thou shalt not eat of it: for in the day that thou eatest thereof thou shalt surely die (Genesis 2:17).**

Hebrew 6:18 points out the impossibility of God telling a lie but in John 8:44 we read where Jesus said Satan **(the devil)** was a murderer from the beginning and abode not in the truth because there is no truth in him. Jesus said not only is he a liar but the father of a liar. He **(Satan)** created a lie as a means of extorting and manipulating the truth. We are aware of the scripture that states, Jesus Christ is the same yesterday, and today, and forever Hebrew 13:8. We should also bear in mind that

Jesus said there was no truth in the devil; what he was from the beginning he still is, a murderer and a liar, and he is still manipulating mankind into thinking they can hide their evil ways and deeds. Hiding or fooling mankind cannot get a person in or out of heaven. It is God that we need to hide from and fool. In trying to do this, I remind you of the words of king David found in Psalm 139:1-12. *O Lord, thou hast searched me, and known* **me.** *Thou knowest my downsitting and mine uprising; thou understandest my thought afar off. Thou compassest my path and my lying down, and art acquainted* **with** *all my ways. For* **there is** *not a word in my tongue,* **but,** *lo O Lord, thou knowest it altogether. Thou hast beset me behind and before, and laid thine hand upon me.* **Such** *knowledge* **is** *too wonderful for me; it is high, I cannot* **attain** *unto it. Whither shall I go from thy Spirit? Or whither shall I flee from thy presence? If I ascend up into heaven, thou,* **art** *there: if I make my bed in hell, behold, thou* **art there.** *If I take the wings of the morning,* **and** *dwell in the uttermost parts of the sea; even there shall thy hand lead me, and thy right hand shall hold me. If I say, surely the darkness shall cover me; even the night shall be light about me. Yea, the darkness hideth not from thee; but the night shineth as the day: and darkness and the light* **are** *both alike* **to thee.** Mankind seems to think as long as they do their evil and lustful deeds under the cover of darkness their secret life style is hidden, therefore it can cause or do no harm to themselves or anyone else. David says no such places exist.

David points out that we cannot hide from God; God even knows the secrets thoughts in our hearts. Hebrew 4:12 says. *"For the word of God* **is** *quick, and powerful, and sharper than any two-edged sword, piercing* *even to the dividing asunder of soul and spirit, and of the joints and marrow, and **is** a discerner of the thoughts and intents of the heart."* God' word is living and powerful. It distinguishes what is natural and what is spiritual in a man and the thoughts and insights of a person heart is exposed through the word. There is no way man can fool God through pretenses or excuses yet so many try. You can find many of these hypocrites among governments and the leadership of our churches today. They use the same methods the devil used on Eve, and people, both men and women, today are misguided by those methods just as easy as Eve was. Eve was beguiled wanting something forbidden for her to have; people today are beguiled wanting to hold on to something they shouldn't keep.

Consider the Patriarch, David, whom God considered to be a man after his own heart, this man wanted to build a house for the Lord but God denied him the privilege of doing so because he had shed blood abundantly and made great wars upon the earth in the sight of God 1 Chronicles 22:8. David understood why he was not an acceptable candidate for building the temple of God and accepted God decision to let his son build the temple. This did not prevent David from gathering material and instructing his son on how the temple should be built. In the same manner today, there are many men and women that have the desire to serve the Lord in the capacity of minister, pastor, elder, bishop, deacon, or etc. for some, there may be things in their past or presence that disqualifies them from leadership but not fellowship among God' people but like in the case of David, this does not mean they shouldn't do all they can to support and help the people of God wherever and whenever they can. There is much work that needs to be done but we need the guidance of the Holy Spirit in order to do the work. This spirit is one that only God can give. It cannot be earned in a seminary school or from performing a weekly sale pitch. Although there are some people who feel one must attend a seminary school in order to be capable of preaching the gospel and there's nothing wrong with attending one. The truth is, one can attend all the seminary schools in the world and not achieve the gift of the Holy Spirit. The disciples of Jesus never attended a seminary school yet they all received the gift of the Holy Spirit because they were approved of God. Attending a seminary school, one can benefit in biblical knowledge; and one must be taught the word of God by some teacher whether it's in a school or by individuals like young Timothy was taught by his mother and grandmother but it will not earn one the Holy Spirit. When God accepts an individual for a position, he seals that individual with the gift of his Holy Spirit. If the person(s) is not acceptable according to God' word, he or she will not be crowned with the spirit of God.

There're those who would have you believe there are none qualified according to scriptural qualifications today to preach, teach, or to do ministry according to God' word. This belief is a lie. If God' words point out the characteristic qualifications a person must have in order to be a leader of God people, there are still people in the world today qualified according to scripture. We, as Christians, should know without a doubt that God does not lie. I've found that people usually judge others by their own life style. If a man is unfit to preach the word of God, his life style as well as the fruit he bears will be manifested. God has a way of caring for his own; he has promised to take care of his children needs as long as they stay connected to the vine (which is Jesus Christ). If we're God,' then our needs will be provided; but if we're not God' born again children, nothing that we do will meet our needs.

The Apostle Paul was a good example of a person attending a seminary school and not having the gift of the Holy Spirit. He was well educated above his peers in the scriptures and wanted to serve God. With all that he had learned from the teachings of men, without the Holy Spirit, spiritually, he was still not equipped to lead God people. Ignorantly, he destroyed all that called on the name of the Lord Jesus Christ, thinking he was serving God. He meant well but like many that are in the pulpits today just meaning well and doing what they think is right will not lead them nor others to the Lord. John 4:24 says that God is a spirit and those who worship Him must worship Him in spirit and in truth. To worship means to serve, no man or woman can serve God without the spirit of God dwelling within him/her.

Earlier I mentioned that God requires the same thing today as he did from the beginning. Look at the man, Cain; he wanted to please God with his offering but there was something wrong with his offering and God had no respect for it. This made Cain angry but God said unto him if you do well, will you not be accepted? And if you do not well, sin lies at the door Genesis 4: 3-6. A God fearing leader has nothing to fear from his/her congregation. If the people are fed the true and healthy word of God, they will grow spiritually in word and love but if they receive not the true word of God, divisions and chaos will eventually erupt among the congregation. Leaders can feed their congregation gossip for just so long. Soon the people will grow weary of listening to the same old relic and the congregation will start declining. To a God fearing leader, a decline in his /her congregation should question his/her standings as an efficient and qualified leader but to a hireling, as long as he/she receives his/her salary and lustful desires, it would have no effect on his/her conscience.

Today, there are too many wannabes in God sanctuaries. They realize few people know the word of God or are interested in knowing the word. Therefore, all one need is the knowledge of salesmanship. Few people can distinguish between gossip and the gospel, so whatever is said is accepted with the listeners not being the wiser. 2 Timothy 3:16 says "all scripture **(the sacred writings contained in the Old and new Testaments combined, God's revelation) is** given by inspiration of God, and **is** profitable **(beneficial)** for doctrine **(teaching),** for reproof **(a cutting rebuke for misconduct),** for correction **(punishment designed to restore),** for instruction **(imparting knowledge to others)** in righteousness **(uprightness before God)**: that the man of God may be perfect**(complete: meaning capable or proficient, skillful)**, thoroughly furnished **(completely equipped: meaning fully prepared)** unto all good works." If one studies the word, he/she will eventually come to the knowledge of the truth and be able to distinguish between what is God word and what is misconception. The belief that one can earn salvation through joining themselves to the attachment of a building of wood, stone, brick, metal, or dirt, is a grave misconception. God does not accept us or what we have to offer any old way. If one desires the gift of salvation, one must seek to be a member of the church that Christ built and continues to expand. A church not made by human hands but one that exist in the heart **(mind)** of all those that truly believe in the Lord Jesus Christ. *Know ye not that ye are the temple of God,* **that** *the Spirit of God dwelleth in you? If any man defile the temple of God, him shall God destroy; for the temple of God is holy, which* **temple** *ye are. Let no man deceive himself. If any man among you seemeth to be wise in this world, let him become a fool, that he may be wise 1 Cor. 3:16-18.* A building is a permanent structure that remains the same day after day. It cannot think; expansion or growth can only come to pass by the use of men physical hands. The church is a living organism that has feelings of love and mercy and continues to grow in wisdom and understanding all guided by the spirit of God. We must do all according to his word in deeds, life changing, and love. If any man be in Christ, according to scripture, he is a new creature. This means he is one that does things and patterns his life according to God word and not his own beliefs or formal life style. People cannot make God accept them if he has not chosen them.

In the role of spiritual leadership, first Timothy 3: 1-13 points out that if a man **(If a Man, it does not say if anyone)** desires the office of leadership then he must **(not should)** reply to what is contained within scripture. If a man desires to serve the Lord in the position of bishop or deacon, the scripture tells him what he has to do to prepare to be acceptable to the Lord. Desire alone is not enough, his life style, character, heart, as well as his knowledgeable ability must also be acceptable unto the Lord. One cannot serve the Lord people without the gift of the Holy Spirit. First Corinthians 4: 2 says it is required in stewards that one be found faithful.

If we search the scriptures, beginning with Adam and Eve, we'll find that faithfulness was and is still a virtue God requires in all that are placed over the leadership of his creation or people. At the beginning of the New Testament church Act 6: 1-7, honesty, faithfulness, and the Holy Spirit were necessary requirements for leadership. God has never and would never place his people in the hands of an unsaved leader. What is an unsaved leader? You'll find some of them listed in Galatians 5: 19-21, Ephesians 5: 3-6, Roman 1:18-32, and first Corinthians 6: 9-10 just to name a few. Can people guilty of these sins be saved? Yes they can. In fact, first Corinthians 6:11 points out that some of the Corinthian Christians were once guilty of the sins listed in verses nine through ten but they had turned from their evil ways and been washed in the blood of the Lamb. Now, they were traveling a path of righteousness. This tells us that a person can change and must change if he/she desires to be saved. The pulpit is not the place for an unsaved person. Jesus said if the blind lead the blind both shall fall into the ditch Matthew 15:14. That leads me to this question; how can the unsaved teach the unsaved how to be saved less they both wind up being loss?

There's an old proverb that says "he who knows and knows that he knows that he knows is wise but he who knows not and knows not that he knows not is a fool." Lately there has been an added version to that proverb that says "he who knows not and knows that he knows not but pretends he knows in order to influence others or to satisfy his selfish greed is unaware that his satanic disguise will eventually come to the light." It is good for one to have a desire to serve but with that desire to serve one should keep in mind the words Joshua said to ancient Israel concerning promises made toward serving God (Joshua 24:14-22). *Be not deceived* **(mislead)** *God is not mocked* **(one to defy and make futile)** *for whatsoever a man soweth* **(spread through words and deeds),** *that shall he also reap* **(be rewarded; blessings for good: cursing for evil) Galatians 6:7.** Our God has placed before us life and death, blessings and cursing and given us the choice to choose our destiny Deut.30:19.

We're blessed to have a promise keeping God watching over us. He is one we can always depend on. His words of truth are not like those of men; his' are always faithful. We know from scripture that God cannot lie so we can without doubts depend on what he says and promises. Being his children, we should believe with confident that our heavenly father will always take care of his children. His inspired words confirm that in Mt. 6:31-33, Luke. 12:27-32, and Phil.4:19. Keep in mind that these scriptures declare that he knows what we have need of and he will provide for our needs and bless us with many of our wants. In fact, if we would be true to ourselves, we'd realize that it's not our needs that keep us in a bind but our uncontrollable wants. If we were satisfied with our needs, we would have fewer sleepless nights and stressful days.

According to James 2:17, faith can only be justified by one' works. Because of Abraham's belief in God, it was imputed **(attributed)** unto him for righteousness. Righteousness means doing and living an upright life before God and men. Doing the things that are right means being obedient to God words. Jesus said "if a man loves me **(speaking of himself),** he will keep my words: and my father will love him, and we will come unto him,

(they will come in the person of the Holy Spirit) and make our abode with him Jn.14:23." 1 John says God' love was manifested through the giving of His Son, Jesus Christ, to die for our sins that we might have a right to the tree of life. God love was and is a love that is plain not only through what he has done but by what he continues to do in our lives daily. The scripture declares that God is love and, if we love one another, the world will see that love dwells in us too.

Introduction

The origin of sin

Sin is the transgression of God's law. With humankind, it began in the garden of Eden after the serpent deceived Eve to defy God' law by eating the fruit from the forbidden tree. She then perceived to talk her husband into eating it also. This is confirmed by scripture.(*Genesis 3:17) and unto Adam he said, because thou hast hearkened **(listened)** unto the voice of thy wife, (it's not known what Eve said unto Adam but it was convincing enough to get him to also defy God' law.) and hast eaten of the tree, of which I commanded thee, saying, thou shalt not eat of it: cursed is the ground for thy sake; in sorrow shalt thou eat of it all the days of thy life.* Some critics will argue that Eve was not accountable because she didn't know the law; they say the law was given to Adam not Eve so no sin was committed until Adam ate the fruit. Look at Genesis 3:1b-3. *And he **(the serpent)** said unto the woman, yea, hath God said, ye shall not eat of every tree of the garden? And the woman **(Eve)** said unto the serpent, we may eat of the fruit of the trees of the garden: but of the fruit of the tree which is in the midst of the garden, God hath said, ye shall not eat of it, neither shall ye touch it, lest ye die.* There it is as plain as day! Eve acknowledged with her own mouth that God had commanded them not to eat or touch the fruit of the forbidden tree. She was aware of the penalty; she was aware of the commandment. Whether she heard God' commandment from Adam or from God himself, the facts is she knew the law and she, after being deceived by the serpent that God had lied, willingly broke that law. According to what she said with her own mouth, all that either one of them had to do was touch the tree for death to come upon them. If Adam had never eaten of the fruit, he might have lived forever but his descendants would still have been born in sin because his wife had broken God' commandment and any seed issued from her womb would also have been of sinful flesh. When we look at Genesis 3: 12-19 we see those involved in the breaking of God' law and how God punished them according to the severity of each of their individual acts. *And He (God) said, who told thee (Adam) that thou wast naked? Hast thou eaten of the tree, whereof I commanded thee that thou shouldest not eat? And the man(Adam) said, the woman(Eve) whom Thou gavest* **to be** *with me, she gave me of the tree, and I did eat* **(willingly he ate; he might have been influenced to eat because he saw nothing had happened to his wife after she had eaten and maybe thought nothing would happen to him. Here he learned, as all of us must learn; God' word means what it says and says what it means in spite of what others say. The conversation they had is not recorded; so no one can say what caused him(Adam) to violate God' commandment by eating the fruit but we do know that his decision to do so was not by force neither was he deceived. However, we know that there was some form of conversation between the woman (Eve) and man (Adam) because God said in verse 17, because thou hast hearkened** (listened) **unto the voice of thy wife.** *In answering God,* notice that Adam did not play the blame game; he simply told exactly what happened. **(Lying or making excuses would not have helped. God knows all and sees all).** He said she **(Eve)** gave it to me and I did eat it.

Adam' weakness or desire to listen to his wife and defy God was no different than many other men weakness toward women. The love of or desire for women has caused men to do many strange things throughout the course of history. Not even the strongest man that ever lived could refrain himself from giving in to women. Consider what Samson did in Judges 14:15-18 and Judges the sixteenth chapter. There was also Solomon, the wisest man that ever lived and even he, with all his wisdom, was not able to refrain from giving in to his strange but beautiful wives. He built them temples for their idol gods and even found himself following after them1 Kings 11:1-8. Nehemiah 13:26b in speaking of Solomon says *"yet among many nations was there no king like him, who was beloved of his God, and God made him king over all Israel: nevertheless even him did outlandish women cause to sin"*. Even in these modern days, we see men who will do strange things to have or entertain a desirable woman. They will steal, rob, kill, deny family, or whatever it takes to secure the love of a beautiful woman. The scripture says the love of money is the root of all evil. For a man, the lust for women must be a close second.

Now let's go back to Genesis and see where God questions Eve. *(Verse 13) and the Lord God said unto the woman **(Eve)**, what is this that thou hast done?* Notice, God did not consider her innocent. His question expresses the severity of her action. *And the woman **(Eve)** did not deny her wrong but said, the serpent beguiled **(tricked)** me, and I did eat.* The serpent, who was wise and crafty, allowed Satan to use him then Satan through him appealed to what was in the woman' heart and triggered her desires to override God' commandment. Go back to verse 6. *And when the woman **(Eve)** saw that the tree **was*** *good for food, and that it **was** pleasant to the eyes, and a tree to be desired to make **one** wise, she took of the fruit thereof, and did eat, and gave also unto her husband with her; and he did eat.* Now, let's continue with verse 14. *And the Lord God said unto the serpent, Because thou hast done this, thou art cursed above every beast of the field; upon thy belly shalt thou go, and dust shalt thou eat all the days of thy life:* the serpent was more subtle **(cunning, crafty, clever, and insidious)** than any beast of the field which the Lord God had made. Satan knows what and who to use to get our attention. He knows and has made a fool out of the wisest of humans. Though he will use the simple minded also, he prefer using those who are wise and those in leadership positions because they have a greater influence on others. He has and will use any and all within his means to interrupt or misuse God' people or service. Look at *verse 16. Unto the woman **(Eve)** he said, I will greatly multiply thy sorrow **(increase her grief, sadness, and regrets, for what she had done and add pain in her childbirth)** and thy conception; in sorrow **(distress)** thou shalt bring forth children; and thy desire **shall be** to thy husband. And he **(Adam)** shall RULE over thee **(Eve)**.*

> Seeds sowed are reaped
> After skeletons awake
> Darkness comes to light

In 1 Cor.11:3 the scripture says *"but I would have you know, that the head of every man is Christ; and the head of every woman **is the** man; and the head of Christ **is** God"*. Verses 7-9 go on to say *"for a man indeed ought not to cover **his** head, forasmuch as he is the image and glory of God: but the woman is the glory of the man. For the man is not of the woman; but the woman of the man.*

Neither was the man created for the woman; but the woman for the man".

This relationship between man and woman was never changed by God. You've had the critic to say, God took the rib from man' side because he wanted man and woman to walk side by side but there's no reference in scripture to support such a saying. God said it was not good for man to dwell alone, so he made man a helpmeet **(a fit mate sufficient for helping man not overseeing or sharing equal partnership)**. For the woman' part in breaking God' commandment, sorrow and pains were added to her body and life. For the serpent' punishment, he was condemned to eating dirt and traveling upon his belly all the days of his life. For the man' part, he was not personally cursed but the ground was cursed instead and he **(man)** in sorrow **(regret)** would have to till and eat of the ground all the days of his life. The serpent and the woman were the two main influential perpetrators of breaking God' commandment: The serpent under the influence of Satan did it to cause chaos. The woman did it out of greed for human pleasures. The man **(Adam)** seems to have done it to please his wife. There have never been any doubt of the serpent' and Adam' guilt but many fail to acknowledge the woman' guilt. Let's turn to 1Timothy 2:14. *And Adam was not deceived, but the woman* **(Eve)** *being deceived was in the transgression* **(sin)**. There it is in plain English! The woman was in the sin; she was the first to break the commandment of God. Adam willingly listening to his wife became partaker to her sin. This by no means excuses Adam from breaking God' law because he had the choice of refusing his wife and remaining obedient to God' commandment. What Adam did was wrong but because he was influenced by his wife his body was not personally cursed as the serpent and Eve' were. Instead, the ground was cursed and from that day forward he would have to till the ground for survival. Before the down fall of man and woman, God provided all that they could ever need or want without their intervention.

One of the greatest faults of mankind today is rejecting the order of things that God has set in place. God set things in the order he wanted to for a reason. It is not man or woman place to question that order but to follow that order. In Romans 9:20-21, we find these words. *"Nay but, O man, who art thou that repliest against God? Shall the thing formed say to Him that formed it, why hast thou made me thus? Hath not the potter power over the clay; of the same lump to make one vessel unto honor, and another unto dishonor"?* God declares in Isaiah 55:8 *"For My thoughts are not your thoughts, neither are your ways My ways. For as the heavens are higher than the earth, so are My ways higher than your ways, and My thoughts than your thoughts."* The order that God has set things in Mankind has no authority to challenge or change but to follow.

Many people live their lives based upon heresy. They rarely take the time to consult God' word to see if those things they hear or have heard are true. There're those who seem satisfied with what mama, the preacher, or some other person(s) they have confident in, say. When we stand before our judge at the last day, we'll have to give an account of the things we've done or have not done. We won't be able to hide behind what someone else said for an excuse. We're told to search the scriptures for ourselves 2Tim. 2:15, John 8:31-32, John 5:39, 1Thes 5:21, 2 Cor. 13:5. Every man, woman, boy, and girl who is serious about their salvation should take the time to be

assured they're following the word of God and not heresy.
Disobedient and rejection of God' order that he set forth
for mankind have brought the wrath of God upon the
world many times over yet mankind refuses to
acknowledge guilt for the wrongs and chaos they have
caused.

When we acknowledge the changing and annulling
of God' commandments and statures that our cities,
states, and federal law makers are denying and changing
to fit their evil ways and desires one after the other, it
should be evident that mankind is developing the attitude
of Satan when he pledged to over throw the government
of the eternal God (Isaiah 14:12-17). Changing God' laws
will and have brought evil upon individual families as well
as the world in general. Just as Satan must someday pay
for his part in deceiving the world, each individual person
will have to pay for his/her mistakes and sins also. Wrong
doings never breed good deeds. It is not our ways or
thoughts that can or will gain us salvation but our ways
and thoughts that are contrary to God's ways and
thoughts can and will lead us to hell. God' word says what
it means and means what it says. The wages of sin is death
but the gift of God is eternal life through his Son Jesus
Christ (Roman 6:23). Search the scriptures; know whom
you're following. Everlasting life is offered to us freely but
so is everlasting damnation.

Table of Contents

Why Are There So Many Divisions In The Church Today?

Answer: Because of mankind' disobedient to God' word:
Proverbs 29:2 states *"when the righteous are in authority, the people rejoice: but when the Wicked beareth rule, the people mourn.* God' word clearly outlines the qualification for church leaders in Acts 6:3 and 1Timothy 3:1-13. Churches today want to choose people according to their liking and ignore God written words. When their selections falter, they then want to pray to God to straighten or fix them up. In Hosea 4:6 we read, *my people are destroyed for lack of knowledge: because thou hast rejected knowledge, I will also reject thee, that thou shalt be no priest to me: seeing thou hast forgotten the law of thy God, I will also forget thy children.* Disobedient will surely bring God' punishment down upon us just as it did for Adam and Eve and we shall reap the consequences thereof. The church is the body of Christ; we cannot use carnal mined people for church leaders if we ever hope to keep our congregation in harmony with each other. Unfaithful people are what caused the disturbance among the church at its birth in Acts 6:1 and we're still placing unconverted people in leadership today reassuring us of the same disturbance as it did in the church of Acts 6:1.

It is a sad thing to see yet it is true. Leaders who say they've been called, whether they're called by God or not, will gain followers. People don't seem interested enough in their salvation to take the time to see what God says about one who has truly been called. You cannot determine a person godly worth **(capability)** by one scripture. Second Peter one and twenty tells us that no prophecy **(inspired foretelling of events)** of the scripture is of any private interpretation **(making the unknown known)**. No man can make the scripture justify his life' desires or wants. All scriptures, according to second Timothy three sixteen and seventeen, are given by the inspiration **(the divine and inspired wisdom of God)** of God not only for the benefit of equipping but correcting the man of God and showing his worth in all things and ways to the eyes of others.

The whole duty of man is to fear God and keep his commandments Eccl.12:13b. Samuel said in 1 Samuel 15:22b *to obey* **is** *better than sacrifices,* **and** *to hearken than the fat of rams.* If we ever hope to dissolve the divisions in the church, we must return to God' word and follow his instructions. Isaiah 40:8 declares; the grass withereth, the flower fadeth: but the word of our God shall stand forever. It **(the bible)** is our guiderail to keep us from falling and it was written for our example. The apostle Peter tells us in 2 Peter 1:20-21 *knowing this first that no prophecy of the scripture is of any private interpretation. For the prophecy came not in old time by the will of man but holy men of God spake* **as they were** *moved by the Holy Ghost.*   If we believe that holy men of God wrote the scriptures as they were moved by the Holy Ghost, we should follow the doctrines they left in place as being God inspired and approved. Jesus said of himself, I am the way, the truth, and the life: no man cometh unto the father, but by me (St. John 14:6). He is the only way to eternal life. He further said in verses 23 and 24, *if a man loves me, he will keep my words: and my Father will love him, and we will come unto him, and make our abode with him* **(this is done through the entering of The Holy spirit).**

*He that loveth me not keepeth not **(does not follow)** my sayings and the word which ye hear is not mine, but the Father's which sent me.*

We're faced with a choice. We can follow God' word and live and worship in harmony or we can continue following the ways of men which lead to destruction. Isaiah prophesied concerning the past and present generations of so-called Christian people (St. Mark 7:6-9). *This people honoreth me with **their** lips, but their heart is far from me. Howbeit in vain do they worship me, teaching **for** doctrines the commandments of men for laying aside the commandment of God, ye hold the tradition of men, **as** the washing of pots and cups: and many other such like things ye do. And he said unto them, full well ye reject the commandment of God, that ye may keep your own tradition.*1 John 2:4 say, *he that saith, I know him **(God)**, and keepeth not his commandments, is a liar, and the truth is not in him.*

If we reject God' choices, God will reject us and our choices. Consider the case of Esau in Hebrew 12:16-17, *lest there **be** any fornicator, or profane person, as Esau, who for one morsel of meat sold his birthright. For ye know how that afterward, when he would have inherited the blessing, he was rejected: for he found no place of repentance, though he sought it carefully with tears.* Remember also King Saul in 1 Sam. 15:26. *And Samuel said unto Saul, I will not return with thee: for thou hast rejected the word of the Lord and the Lord hath rejected thee from being king over Israel.* The Lord is an unchanging God. In Malachi 3:6, we find these words. *"For I **am** the Lord, I change not; therefore ye sons of Jacob are not consumed."*

The Hebrew writer declares that Jesus Christ is the same yesterday, and today, and for ever more Hebrew 13:8.

Just as ancient Israel, Judah, and their kings were rejected by God for rejecting his words and commandments, so are people today. Hosea was inspired by God to write these words. *My people are destroyed for lack of knowledge: because thou hast rejected knowledge, I will also reject thee, that thou shalt be no priest to me: seeing thou hast forgotten the law of thy God, I will also forget thy children.* God endowed men with the Holy Spirit and wisdom to write down his words and commandments so future generations would know how God desires his children to live. If we follow them, we'll find blessings and prosperity. If we reject them, we'll only bring more of what we're experiencing today down on us and we'll only have ourselves to blame. If we desire harmony in worship, we need only be obedient to God and his word.

St. Mark 10:8-9 states that when a man and woman are joined together in marriage, they are no longer twain but one flesh. What therefore God hath joined together, let not man put asunder. Whatever God says, inspires, or have holy men put together no man or woman has the right to separate or annul. Keep in mind that Peter said the prophecy came not in old time by the will of man but holy men of God spoke **as they were** moved by the Holy Ghost. This tells us that the scripture is the inspired word of God written by holy Prophets and Apostles. In Isaiah 55:11, God tells us that the word that goes forth out of his mouth shall not return unto him void but shall prosper **in the thing** whereto he sent it. Yet men have seen fit to ignore the written word of God and established their own personal agenda as to what is right and what is wrong. Because so few people read their bibles, they are easily misled. As long as man refuses to follow and obey God' word, heresies and divisions will continue to spread among our church congregations. If we want the divisions to cease, we must return to God' word, select God inspired leaders who are of honest report, filled with wisdom, and let the Holy Spirit guide them as they guide and teach us in the ways that God would have us to go. Only through Jesus Christ can we enter through the door into eternal life. Only through following God' words and commandments can we restore harmony back into the church. We can find peace in God' words if we follow them. Denying them can only bring us shame, destruction, and more of what we're faced with in our churches today.

The betrayal of our Lord must stop if we, as Christians, ever hope to end the divisions among our church congregations today. *The thing that hath been, it **is that** which shall be; and that which is done **is** that which shall be done: and **there is** no new **thing** under the sun.* Do you remember reading these words in Eccl.1:9? I bring this scripture to your attention to remind you that whatever we're witnessing today, others have witnessed them at diver times in the past and still others will witness them in the future. Even from the beginning, Satan has found a way to come between people and their obedient to the living God. In St. John 10:9-10a, Jesus said, *"I am the door: by me if any man enters in, he shall be saved, and shall go in and out, and find pasture. The thief **(referring to the devil and his followers)** cometh not, but for to steal, and to kill, and to destroy:"* He **(the devil, by appealing to mankind' lustful desires of the flesh)** destroyed the relationship Adam and Eve had with the living God. He entered the heart of Cain to kill his brother, Abel, David to have Uriah killed trying to cover up his sin, Moses and Aaron to steal God's glory by striking the rock instead of speaking to it, David to number Israel, causing thousands to be destroyed because of his disobedience, Rehoboam to deny wisdom and heed youthful advice which destroyed the united kingdom of Israel, even destroying the spiritual relationship that Judas shared with his Lord and Savior. These things, Satan has devoted his cause too and he continues to use mankind by appealing to their greed, selfishness, lusts, pride, the desire for self praises, and any and all things that causes people to destroy their' and others lives through deceitfulness.

Judas was not the only one to sell out his Lord for the love of money. Countless men and women have and are doing the same, if not worse, today. The love of money and the things it can attain in the world have drawn many away from the faith. The scripture says that those that have coveted after money have erred from the faith and pierced themselves through with many sorrows. The sad thing is many are coveting after the riches of this world and are not aware of the temptations money creates that draws men farther and farther away from the true and living God. The decision every Christian is eventually face with in life is whether he/she will be a friend of the world or a servant of God. No one can be both. 1 John 2:15 says, "Love not the world, neither the things **that are** in the world. If any man loves the world, the love of the father is not in him." (Here the emphasis is put upon the lustful things the world has to offer in comparison to the righteousness of God. We do this often when we put our wants, jobs, families, desires, feelings, homes, cars, education, and worldly pleasures, above our Christian obligations to God and our fellowman). In considering our reasonable obligations to God, we're urged not to be conformed to this world, but be transformed by the renewing of our mind, that we may prove what **is** good and acceptable and the perfect will of God (Romans 12:2). As Christian, whether leaders or followers, our mind should be focused on the things that pertain to righteousness not worldly pleasures. Spiritual transformation is one that begins in the mind and heart and is dedicated to the truths of God; Embraced by the Holy Spirit, the beholder can stand the test of time if he/she allow the spirit to guide and shape his/her thoughts and behaviors.

If I'm Trying To Be A Christian, Does That Count?

Answer: it's not trying; it's trusting that counts. Trying will not get us into heaven' gates. We must overcome our weaknesses and doubts. If the will and desire to succeed are strong enough, the way will be provided.

A drowning man tries with all his might but cannot stay afloat but when he trusts in another he is rescued. No matter how hard you try; you cannot free yourself from Satan grips under your own power. We all need the power of Jesus to overcome the devil. In Matthew 15: 4-5, Jesus said *abide in me, and I in you. As the branch cannot bear fruit of itself, except it abide in the vine; no more can ye, except ye abide in me. I am the vine, ye are the branches: he that abideth in me, and I in him, the same bringth forth much fruit: for without me ye can do nothing.*

On our own, we cannot defeat the wiles of Satan that floods our minds; his is stronger and much wiser than our'. In fact, the scripture says he is wiser than Daniel was Ezek. 28:3. Only Jesus has and can defeat him. In Mark 8:34b-, we read where Jesus said "Whosoever will come after Me, let him deny himself; and take up his cross, and follow Me. But remember also the apostle Paul said in 2 Tim.3:12 all that will live godly in Christ Jesus shall suffer persecution. This tells us that we shall have trials and tribulations but these things are necessary in the life of a Christian to make us stronger. The road to salvation is a rugged road but it is travelable with the help of Jesus. It is not he who tries that wins the crown but the one that continue to the end. As long as we can hear the Lord Jesus' voice, we should never give up. The Hebrew writer said " *wherefore (as the Holy Ghost saith, Today if ye will hear His voice, harden not your hearts, as in the provocation, in the day of temptation in the wilderness Heb.3:7.")*

If one tries to live the Christian life, one can if the desire to live for Christ is stronger than the desire to hold on to the things of the world. God knows every hidden thought of the human mind. He knows when we're sincere; he knows when we're not. Jesus said *"behold, I stand at the door and knock: if any man hear My voice, and open the door, I will come in to him, and will sup with him, and he with Me Rev. 3:20."* As it is not the hearer of the word but the doer of the word that is justified, it is not he who tries but he who lives the Christian life that shall be saved.

In a physical race, only the ones who come in first win the crown. The next two or three following gets recognition but nothing is given to those that come in last. In the spiritual race, everyone that finishes the race gets a crown. It's not how fast or how long one runs the race; what matters is that one finishes the race. One who refuses to run the spiritual race because of unbelief is condemned already because he/she hath not believed in the name of the only begotten Son of God (John 3:18). John 3:16 says, God sent not His Son into the world to condemn the world; but that the world through Him might be saved. Jesus is the only way to eternal life. He shed his blood on the cross that all men, women, boys and girls, would have the right to the tree of life. If one truly wants to live the Christian life; one can if one truly has a love for Jesus and self. If we have a willing mind and make the first step through repentance, Jesus will provide the way; all we have to do is accept Him and His ways to being saved. Once we've truly accepted Jesus and believed in him, we have the promise of eternal life to look forward to if we continue to be faithful until the end. Read St. John the sixteenth chapter. Through reading it, it should set your mind at ease. It is God our Savior' desire that all men be saved first Timothy 2:4.

What Is Tithing?

Answer: Tithing is the giving of the tenth of a person' earnings. In the Old Testament it included basically any and everything that a person raised whether crops or livestock. Money was given as a freewill offering but the tithes was commanded and required by God. The giver of tithes should understand tithing is not a contract to eternal life but an avenue through which one can acquire earthly and spiritual blessings.

The first known mention of tithes were when Abraham gave freely a tenth of the spoil he confiscated from his battle with Chedorlaomer and the kings that were with him Genesis 14:17-20. The second mention is when his grandson, Jacob, promised freely to give a tenth of his earnings to God for his blessing Genesis 28:20-22. Before there was a law, the tithe was freely given as a means of thanking God for his blessings. The beginning of tithes started with Abraham who was the father of the faithful. The church is comprised of the children of faith. Therefore, as the children of faith, we should follow the example of father Abraham. What we give whether it be tithes or offerings, we should give freely as we've proposed in our heart and not by constraint, force, or guilt. This line of thought corresponds with what Paul said in 2 Corinthians 9:6-7. *But this **I say,** he which soweth sparingly **(scanty or little)** shall reap also sparingly; and he which soweth bountifully **(generously)** shall reap also bountifully **(generously)**. every man according as he purposeth in his heart* **(as each individual plans or intends in his or her own heart, not being influenced or forced to do in order to remain a member on some church role book***), so let* *him give; not grudgingly **(without envying or regretful)**, or of necessity **(fate or unavoidable)**; for God loveth a cheerful giver.* When one is forced to give, it is not out of love but by means of coercing. All God gives to us, he gives it freely. What we give to him should be likewise given.

In the New Testament, you'll see no mention of tithes. Remember the New Testament church began on the day of Pentecost. In the gospels of Matthew, Mark, Luke, and John, the people were still under the law. Jesus said he came to fulfill the law not to abolish it. The law was originally given to the nation of Israel as an everlasting law to observe but it was not given to the Gentiles. This law was still in effect during the period Jesus spent on earth in the form of man and he observed it and explained it and its importance. When the Gentiles were accepted as a part of God' church, starting with Cornelius' household that heard the word which Peter preached Acts 10:44-48, it brought questions of concern from the Jerusalem church. But when Peter rehearsed **the matter** from the beginning, and expounded **it** by order unto them (Acts 11:4). Verse 18 goes on to say *when they **(the Jerusalem church leaders)** heard these things, they held their peace, and glorified God, saying, then hath God also to the Gentiles granted repentance unto life. Acts 15: 10 Now therefore why tempt **(test)** ye God, to put a yoke **(burden)** upon the neck of the disciples, which neither our fathers nor we were able to bear. Verse 19 says wherefore my sentence **(judgment)** is, that we trouble not them, which from among the Gentiles are turned to God: but that we write unto them, that they abstain from pollutions of idols, and **from** fornication, and **from** things strangled, and **from** blood.* The law was not forced upon the Gentiles. In the book of St. Luke chapter 18:9-14, Jesus tells a parable of a Pharisee and Publican that went up into the temple to pray. While the Pharisee bragged about his self-righteousness and paying of his tithes, the Publican humbly admitted to what he was and asked for mercy. The Publican' reverence and obedient was considered more important and righteous than the Pharisee' self-righteous altitude of devotional bragging and paying tithes. Whereas there's nothing wrong with paying tithes, the danger many people face today is thinking that the paying of their tithes gains them a pass to salvation in spite of their evil life style. Let's look at what Jesus said in Matthew 23:23 *"woe unto you, scribes and Pharisees, hypocrites! For ye pay tithe of mint and anise and cummin, and have omitted the weightier **matters** of the law, judgment, mercy, and faith: these ought ye to have done, and not to leave the other undone."*

Today many people pay tithes but they avoid the more needful things of service. Some even pretend to pay tithes in order to look good before others without realizing the danger of lying to God. We're blessed for what we freely give for the furthering of the gospel and aide to our fellow man not for what we pretend to give or do. Remember what happened to Ananias and Sapphira for lying to God by pretending to give all that they received from the sale of a possession Acts 5:1-10. Also, we must keep in mind what Jesus said to the scribes and Pharisees considering the most weightier and important things. For the faithful those things include love, faith, mercy, forgiveness, prayer, and keeping God' word, *"let us hear the conclusion of the whole matter: fear God, and keep his commandments: for this **is** the whole **duty** of man Ecclesiastes 12:133."*

Paul told the Corinthian church to give according to the way they've been blessed. *Every man according as he purposeth **(aims or intentional plans to do so)** in his heart, **so let him give:** not grudgingly, **(without resentment)** or of necessity **(by force or coercion):** for God loveth a cheerful giver 2 Cor. 6:7.* Whatever we do or give concerning the church should be done on a free will basic. 1 Peter 5:1—3 even points out that the leadership role of the church should be taken on willingly and not by compulsion. When we back up to verse six, we read. *But this **I say,** he which soweth sparingly **(gives little)** shall reap also sparingly **(little);** and he which soweth bountifully **(gives much, money, knowledge, service, helps, or etc.)** shall reap also bountifully.* These verses, written to the members of the New Testament church, tell us that our giving should be done willfully not out of restraint and that our giving whatever it or they may be has a result on our blessings received. Matthew 7:2 states *for with what judgment **(criticism)** ye judge, ye shall be judged: and with what measure **(amount)** ye mete, **(give)** it shall be measured **(returned)** to you again.*

Through wisdom Solomon says to us *cast thy bread upon the waters: for thou shalt find it after many days.* No good deeds or gifts of love go unnoticed by God. In fact, Jesus said in St. Luke 18:29-30 ' verily I say unto you, there is no man that hath left house, or parents, or brethren, or wife, or children, for the kingdom of God's sake, who shall not receive manifold more in this present time, and in the world to come life everlasting." The giving of tithes was not instituted by God as a means of giving salvation but as a mean of caring for those that oversees God service and as a means of providing for the poor and needed. It was never designed as a means to making men rich. The tithes system worked similar like our tax system today. It was put in place to take care of all the temple workers that cleaned the temple and assisted the people concerning sacrifices and other services in the temple. The priests also were recipient of the tithes as well as the poor and stranger that came in to dwell among the Israelites.

Deuteronomy 14:22 states the law of the tithes. *Thou shalt truly tithe all the increase of thy seed, (he didn't say money.) that the field bringeth forth year by year. And thou shalt eat before the Lord thy God, in the place which he shall choose to place his name there, the tithe of thy corn, of thy wine, and of thine oil, and the firstling of thy herds and of thy flocks; that thou mayest learn to fear the Lord thy God always.*

Tithing is a good thing but it should never be forced upon a person to give nor should a person be shamed into giving. Whatever the amount given, it should be given freely. However, there're many things money can't buy that people are in need of. Religious leaders should teach their congregation to give out of the abundant of things they have whether it's time, money, knowledge, friendship, clothing, material blessings or etc. James 2:15-16 says *"if a brother or sister be naked, and destitute (in need) of daily food, and one of you say unto them, depart in peace, be ye warmed and filled; notwithstanding ye give them not those things which are needful to the body; what doth it profit?"* **What this says is, if people are hungry and in need of raiment and you give them food and let them warm by your fire but send them away naked, you've half done the job; the people needs have not been met. Another example is, if a person is on his sick bed unable to prepare his own meal and you go in and pray for him** *but does nothing for his empty stomach, you have not administered to his needs. In our giving, in our helping, let us give what is needed but do it freely from the heart. If a man needs food, give him food alone with your prayer. If a man needs a friend, go to him and offer him comfort, don't send a card in your stead. It is true; we should always pray for one another but let us not forget to administer to one another' needs not one another' wants or give for conscience sake. God gave his Son freely to the world that the world through him might be saved. Jesus died freely for the sins of mankind that they once again might have a chance to the tree of life. All of mankind' gifts should be from the heart freely given out of love for God and the support and concern for all of God' creation; we and all that we have belong to God. As God is not selfish in his giving, nothing that we do as Christians should be done selfishly or for vain glory. All that we do, all that we give, should be freely done out of love.* Giving is a part of the Christian profession. As God has given to us, we should likewise give to our fellowman but in our giving and all that we do let us heed the words of proverbs 4:7 which says, wisdom **is** the principal thing; **therefore** get wisdom: and with all thy getting get understanding.

Can A Person Be Lost Once They're Saved?

Answer: No, but how do we determine if we're saved? Romans 8:1 say" *there is therefore now no condemnation to them which (ARE) in Christ Jesus, who walks not after the flesh, but after the spirit."*

The person must walk after the spirit in order to avoid condemnation. Jesus says in St. John 6:37 *"all that the father giveth me shall come to me; and him that cometh to Me I will in no wise cast out."* However, you must be able to determine whether you're in Christ before you get relaxed with this question. If a person is in Christ Jesus, that person does not practice sin any more in his/her life. If sin is still within a person' life, that person cannot be in Christ and if the person is not in Christ the person is not saved. As long as you remain faithful unto the Lord, he will not leave or forsake you but this doesn't stop you from leaving or forsaking him as ancient Israel did on many occasions. Keep in mind the knowledge of the fact that no man has any saving power, only Jesus can save. Neither of us truly knows the heart of anyone else; therefore, we cannot truthfully say if a person is saved or lost. We can only testify to what we believe by what we see, hear, or have seen.

Salvation is something we should take serious. Therefore, we need to know for sure whether we've reached that goal or headed in the right or wrong direction. In St. John 5:39 we read where Jesus said *"search the scriptures; for in them ye think ye have eternal life: and they are they which testify of me."* Don't just think you're saved because you've heard it said. Search the scriptures for yourself and compare them with your present way of life then judge for yourself whether you're in Christ or still holding on to your formal sins. If we've reached the goal of being saved, our salvation is sure as long as we remain faithful. The Apostle Paul left these words on record in Romans 8:35-39. *"Who shall separate us from the love of Christ? Shall tribulation, or distress, or persecution, or famine, or nakedness, or peril, or sword? As it is written, for thy sake we are killed all the day long; we are accounted as sheep for the slaughter. Nay, in all these things we are more than conquerors through him that loved us. For I am persuaded, that neither death, nor life, nor angels, nor principalities, nor powers, nor things present, nor things to come, nor heights, nor depth, nor any other creature, shall be able to separate us from the love of God, which is in Christ Jesus our Lord."*

Going down taking the preacher' hand doesn't mean you're saved; being baptized doesn't mean you're saved; assembling with a church congregation every Sunday doesn't mean you're saved; just because you pay tithes doesn't mean you're saved; having your name on some church role book doesn't mean you're saved; taking part in the communion service doesn't mean you're saved; being able to quote bible scriptures doesn't mean you're a Christian or that you're saved. Just because you believe there's a God in the heavens, it doesn't mean you're saved; though, all of the above are attributions of a Christian, they cannot confirm that one is saved.

The devil is also one that believes and knows there's a God in the heavens. James 3:19 says *"thou believest that there is one God; thou doest well: the devils also believe, and tremble.* The devil also knows and can quote scriptures. This is confirmed by the following verses. *Then the devil taketh Him (Jesus) up into the holy city, and setteth him on a pinnacle of the temple. And saith unto Him, if Thou be the Son of God, cast Thyself down: for it is written, (Psalms 91:11-12) He shall give His angels charge concerning Thee: and in their hands they shall bear Thee up, lest at any time Thou dash Thy foot against a stone Matthew 4:5-6, St. Luke 4:1-11.*

2 Cor. 5:17-18 states *"therefore if any man be in Christ, he is a new creature: (there it is in plain language). (If any man be in Christ, the change will be noticed. People will see the difference; you, yourself, will notice the difference. The old you will be gone. You'll find yourself with a new attitude toward life, God, and other) all things are become new. And all things are of God, who hath reconciled us to himself by Jesus Christ, and hath given to us the ministry of reconciliation.* If a person is saved, the change will be noticed in his/her life style. His/her talk and walk will be completely different from his/her formal life style. Just as a tree is known by the fruit it bears, a Christian is known by the fruit he/she bears. A Christian' fruit is love, peace, mercy, meekness, and faith, shown through his/her true and righteous works.

If one is saved, his/her old ways of life will be a thing of the past. The thought of engaging in back alley dice games will no longer appeal to him/her. Having a desire to take part in wild exotic parties will no longer exist, being a busy body, throwing stone for stone, these things and things like them when one accepts the Lord, he/she puts away. So read, study, meditate, and pray, for guidance, understanding, and strength to help you determine whether you're in Christ endowed with the gift of The Holy Spirit. Don't be like Mother Eve and lose your chance of eternal life being deceived by the desire to attain or hold on to worldly lusts and desires. I urge you also to consider the case of Judas Iscariot, one of the twelve disciples Jesus sent out to heal the sick, cleanse the lepers, raise the dead, and cast out devils. He had obtained part of the ministry of salvation but he was guide to them that took Jesus and lost it Matt. 10: 1-8, Acts 1:16-17. He **(Judas)** committed the unpardonable sin. He willfully sinned against his Lord and Christ for the love of money. After coming to grips to what he had done, he could no longer live with himself so he went out and hung himself. After being with the Lord day and night for several years, listening to his teaching, eye witnessing his miracles, and receiving the Holy Spirit from him, which gave him the power to cast out devils, heal the sick, give sight to the blind, and restore strength back into the limbs of the lame, Judas tasted the gift of the Lord and new for sure he was the Son of God. The one thing that stood between Judas and his salvation was his love for the almighty dollar. Like Judas, we're given the choice of choosing between The Almighty God and the almighty dollar. The almighty dollar makes possible a few pleasures for a short period of time on earth and has no control over death but the almighty God makes possible eternal life with unlimited pleasures in the New Jerusalem without endings.

By what we've learned of Judas, we see that a person can be on his/her way to being saved and of his/her own free will turn and go in a different direction. If the change is willingly, after one has tasted the true gift of God, it will be impossible for that person to receive repentance again. According to Hebrew 6:4-6, once a person gives up his/her chance for salvation he/she cannot regain his/her formal chance for salvation. So you cannot accept the Lord as your savior and live just any old way without being expected to lose something. Once you start on the road to salvation, be true to yourself and God alike. Salvation is an awful thing to lose. It would be a frighten night mare to think that you're saved and ends up in hell' fire. Therefore, once we start on the road to life, we should continue on till the end of life. Consider the words of Jesus in Matthew 10:22 and Mark 13:13;" *and ye shall be hated of all* **men** *for my name's sake: but he that endureth* **(persists)** *to the end shall be saved." Also he says in Matthew 24:12-13, "and because iniquity* **(sin)** *shall abound, the love of many shall wax* **(become)** *cold. But he that shall endure unto the end, the same shall be saved."* And finally, in Revelation 2:26, he says; "and he that over cometh, and keepeth **(continues to do)** *My works unto the end, to him will I give power over the nations:"* further he says in Rev. 2:10 *"fear none of those things which thou shalt suffer: behold, the devil shall cast* **some** *of you into prison, that ye may be tried* **(tested);** *and ye shall have tribulations* **(persecutions)***ten days: be thou faithful unto death, and I will give thee a crown of life."* We'll only truly know that we're saved when Jesus calls us up to meet him in the air and carries us to his heavenly kingdom. Once we're there, we'll have no need to fear the fires of hell. God, Jesus, and The Holy Ghost, these three are one 1 John 5:7 and the scripture says that God cannot lie. In reviewing the parable of the rich man and Lazarus, we see where the rich man was told that there will be a great gulf fixed so that those in heaven cannot cross over to visit or ease the pain of those in hell and those in hell cannot cross over to enjoy the comfort of those in heaven Luke 16: 25-26.

(2 Cor. 5:17) if any man/woman/boy/girl be in Christ he/she is a new creature. John 3:14 says *"We know that we have passed from death unto life, because we love the brethren. He that loveth not **his** brother abideth in death.* Again he says in John 4:12-13 *"No man hath seen God at any time. If we love one another, God dwelleth in us, and his love is perfected in us. Hereby know we that we dwell in him, and he in us, because he hath given us of his spirit."* If the spirit of God dwells within us, we have eternal life within us.

1 John3:7-10 *"little Children, let no man deceive you: he that doeth righteousness is righteous, even as He is righteous. He that committeth sin is of the devil: for the devil sinneth from the beginning. For this purpose the Son of God was manifested, that He might destroy the works of the devil. Whosoever is born of God doth not commit **(practice)** sin; for His seed remaineth in him; and he cannot sin, because he is born of God."* Paul, in 2 Cor.5:17, offers further proof by saying if any man be in Christ he is a new creature. He/she no longer does or wants to do the things he/she did in the past. One' desire after being saved is to please the Lord in service and life style. If you still have an over whelmed desire to engage in the things of the world, something is wrong with your commitment. One cannot serve God and mammon **(the devil)** too. (Matthew 6:24). Don't fool yourself; you cannot love those you want to love and hate or dislike those you want to hate or dislike. When we're able to love all men, women, boys, and girls, in spite of their differences, we know we're on the right road to salvation. Once we're on the right road, we should be careful not to turn around or betray the trust of the God that has done so much for us. In fact Hebrew 3:14

says, *for we are made partakers **(partners)** of Christ, if we hold the beginning of our confidence steadfast **(firm)** unto the end.* The overall view of this scripture seem to point to the fact that one must continue doing the things that are right and pleasing in the sight of God until the end in order to be saved. The apostle John says in I John; we know that we've passed from death to life when we're able to love the brethren. This love must exceed lip service and mouth confession. It must be a truth that comes from the heart. Truth cannot be hidden; it was never meant to be hidden. Jesus Christ' death on the cross was not done in secret; it was open for the world to witness. Christianity is not a thing to be hidden but one to be openly lived glorifying the God of creation. It must be seen in our daily walk. We cannot put Christ on and off. Either we're Christ' or we're not and the world should be able to see the Christ in us all of the time. Don't make the mistake of thinking you're saved because of what others say. Examine the scriptures for yourself and see if your life line up with what the scripture say about being saved.

Can We, Or Do We, Have The Right To Tell Others When They're Wrong?

Answer: Yes we can and yes we do. For Christians, it is our duty to tell others of their faults not wanting them to be loss but we must approach them with the right altitude and we ourselves must be righteous. Consider what Galatians 6:1 says. *"Brethren, if a man be overtaken in a fault, (ye) which are spiritual, restore such a one in the spirit of meekness; considering thyself, lest thou also be tempted."*

This and other scriptures tell us that one should be righteous his/her self before trying to tell others of their faults. Jesus said unto Peter when thou art CONVERTED strengthen thy brethren St. Luke 22:32b. Some people love to point out others faults and try to tell them what is right and what is wrong but Jesus reminds us in St. Luke 6:41-42 and St. Matthew 7:3-5, if we have a beam within our own eyes, how can we see clearly how to help our brother or sister to get the mote out of their eyes. He tells us first straighten up our own lives that others may see us as an example of what we're talking about. A blind man or woman has no ability to lead or guide another blind man or woman since both are in the same condition. He/she must rely on someone with sight to guide them in all things.

Whether we're young or old, it is the Christian' duty to follow the example the apostle Paul outlined for young Timothy in 1 Timothy 4:12b." *But be thou an example of the believers, in word, in conversation, in charity, in spirit, in faith, in purity."* He further offers himself in 1 Cor.11:1 up as an example of one following Christ. We, as all Christians, are not to pattern our lives after the scribes and Pharisees Jesus spoke of in Matthew 23:2-4. *".. The scribes and Pharisees sit in Moses seat: all therefore whatsoever they bid you observe, that observe and do; but do not ye after their works; for they say, and do not. For they bind heavy burdens and grievous to be borne, and lay **them** on men's shoulders; but they **themselves** will not move them with one of their fingers:"*

Christians should always heed the words they tell to others and be mindful of what the Scriptures say about those who know to do right and fail to do it in Luke 12: 47. The book of Ezekiel tells us that we must warn a person when he/she is doing wrong. If we don't and the person dies in his/her sin, that person blood will be on our shoulder. There's always a penalty for being disobedient no matter who does it; whether it's to mankind or God. Right is right and wrong is wrong no matter who tells you to do it or not to do it. Jesus said a tree is known by the fruit it bare. You wouldn't go to an apple tree looking to pick a peach. Likewise, you shouldn't expect a hypocrite to provide you with the truth. We should be aware of who or what we're following. Actions speak louder than words. Jesus said in St. John 8:31-32 *"if ye continue in My word, **then** are ye My disciples indeed **(works)**; and ye shall know the truth, and the truth shall make you free."*

As Christians, if we never reach the level where we can tell others of their short comings, we should examine ourselves. *Examine yourselves, whether ye be in the faith; prove your own selves. Know ye not your own selves, how that Jesus Christ is in you, except ye be reprobates* **(ones rejected by God)** *2 Corinthians13:5.* Remember 2 Corinthians 5:17-18 says, *"if any man be in Christ, he is a new creature: all things are of God who hath reconciled us to Himself by Jesus Christ."* If we're in the Lord, we should grow stronger and stronger as we get to know him. Eventually, we'll reach the point, if we continue in his words and commandments, where we can tell and show others truth of God' goodness and loving grace through our' character and life style.

      We should also keep in mind that a person can be a good man in his own sight and in the view point of some other people and yet not be a saved man. Solomon says most men will proclaim everyone his own goodness: but a faithful man who can find (Proverbs 20:6)? Through our faithfulness, others are drawn to Christ but that faithfulness must be shown through our character and life style. Words alone are not convincing enough to draw others to Christ since there're so many pretenders in the world today. Every child of God should seek to live a life that glorifies the Lord that lives within his/her heart. When others see the goodness of God working within us, they too will want to share the God of our lives. It is then we should take the opportunity to tell them of our forgiving Lord and Savior, Jesus Christ.

Once One Becomes A Servant Of God, Will One Still Have A Weakness To Sin?

Answer: Yes you will; as long as you're in your mortal body, worldly desires will pledge your mind. As a Christian, the flesh and spirit will constantly be at war with each other.

Consider what Ecclesiastes 7:20 says." *For there is not a just man upon earth, that doeth good, and sinneth not."* This tells us no matter how righteous we are or how long we've been in the faith, as long as we're in our mortal body, not only will we have the urge but we're going to sin from time to time. We must always keep our mind focused on Jesus to prevent Satan from slipping in leading us astray. Paul said in Romans 7:14-21 *"For we know the law is spiritual: but I am Carnal sold under sin. For that which I do I allow not: for what I would, that do I not; but what I hate, that I do. If then I do that which I would not, I consent unto the law that **it is** good. Now then it is no more I that do it, but sin that dwelleth in me. For I know that in me (that is, in my flesh,) dwelleth no good thing: for to will is present with me; but **how** to perform that which is good I find not. For the good that I would I do not: but the evil which I would not, that I do. Now if I do that I would not, it is no more I that do it, but sin that dwelleth in me. I find then a law, that, when I would do good, evil is present with me. For I delight in the law of God after the inward man: but I see another law in my members, warring against the law of my mind, and bringing me into captivity* *to the law of sin which is in my members. O wretched man that I am! Who shall deliver me from the body of this death? I thank God through Jesus Christ our Lord. So then with the mind I my-self serve the law of God: but with the flesh the law of sin."* Often in our lives, we find ourselves falling weak to the desires of the flesh.

David was said to be a man after God own heart yet he fell weak and committed adultery with Bathsheba. Even the best of us get weak. Jesus in referring to Peter, James, and John, inability to stay awake and watch while he prayed, said unto them "watch ye and pray, lest ye enter into temptation. The spirit truly **is** ready, but the flesh **is** weak." Whether we have a desire to do so or not; circumstances in life will arise. It is when we think we're above sin that deceives us of our frailty of being human.

The old warriors had a saying that an idle mind is the devil' playground; if we keep our minds on the Lord at all times, it will leave little   time to dwell on unchristian like things. As Jesus told his disciples "the spirit is ready but the flesh is weak." We find on a daily basic we have to contend with the weakness of the flesh. This is why we must always keep our mind on Jesus and not allow space for the devil to get our attention. As it was for Jesus and his disciples, prayer is the source of our strength. It gives us the power to accept God will.

In the bread of life,
Faith helps us to over come
In times of weakness

Solomon said what is has already been. Let's consider some of the people before us. The prophet Jonah was probably one of the most powerful preachers of his ere. Because of his envy toward the wicked, he was disobedient toward the mission God sent him on at first. But God had a way of letting him know the word of God will go forward by whom he desires it to go forward by. Jonah was commissioned the second time to go down and preach to Nineveh concerning their wickedness. When Jonah started through that great and lengthy city his message of destruction by God in forty-days was so convincing that from the greatest to the least of the inhabitants of Nineveh went in prayer with sackcloth and ashes repenting and hoping that God would have a change of heart. God saw their conviction and spared them for their change of heart but this angered Jonah. Jonah was a man of God yet his mercy toward others was weak. We should be careful not to let envy cloud our service to others.

First Samuel tells us of David, Israel best loved king, lust for beauty. Even though he was said to be a man after God' own heart, It may not have been his intentions to sin but he did (Second Samuel 11:2-4). His son, Solomon, was the wisest and richest king that ever lived. First king 11:1-8 tells us his love and lust for strange and beautiful women eventually led him to sin against God. And there was Samson, the strongest man that ever live, who's lust for strange women brought him down after breaking the Nazarene' sacred vow.

Moses was the leader of the Israelites that led them out of Egyptian bondage. He was faithful in all his house according to scripture yet anger caused him to sin and it robbed him of his opportunity to lead the Israelites into the promise land (Numbers 20:1-13). And there was

Lot, the nephew of Abraham, who, unknowingly, allowed selfishness to lead him to the destruction of all his possessions and family. And let us not forget Judas, a disciple of Jesus that preached the gospel and casted out devils, and healed many with various diseases. He allowed his uncontrollable lust for money to drive him to betray his and our Lord.

The point I'm trying to make is no matter what you are, whether Christian or nonbeliever, the weakness of the flesh exists. First John 3:9 tells us whosoever is born of God doth not practice sin. For his seed remains in him and he cannot sin because he is born of God, if we allow the devil to enter our lives, he'll sway our thoughts. Therefore, if we live in the spirit, we should walk in the spirit. Our talk should always justify our walk. None of us are immune to sin but with Christ in our lives we can overcome sin. The devil is busy and persuasive but we as Christians serve one that is stronger, merciful, and forgiving, Jesus Christ, our Lord and Savior.

Can Or Will Baptism Save Us?

Answer: Baptism has no saving powers alone by itself. It is however one of the ordinances of the Christian faith and it is something that must be done.

Jesus points out that belief should precede baptism. Mark 16:15-16a. *And he (Jesus) said unto them (his disciples), go ye into all the world, and preach the gospel to every creature. He that believeth and is baptized shall be saved: but he that believeth not shall be damned.* He also says in St. John 3:5 *"verily, verily, I say unto thee, except a man be born of water and of the spirit, he cannot enter into the kingdom of God."* So this tells us baptism is essential for salvation but it has no saving power of his own. Just as faith is dead without works (James 2:20) so baptism is useless without being born of the spirit. As faith and works justified each other, being born of the spirit and water certifies a born again Christian believer's confession.

Baptism is an ordinance that one should go through only after one has been taught and understands the process. Baptism should take place after one has accepted Jesus as his/her Lord, not before. Notice when the Ethiopian Eunuch understood and believed the word it was then and only then that he was a candidate for baptism Acts 8:26-38. At Cornelius house, after they had heard the word preached by Peter and believed in their hearts, the Holy Spirit fell upon them. Peter then asked the brethren, can any man forbid water, that these should not be baptized, which have received the Holy Ghost as well as we? Paul after acknowledging the Lord Jesus Christ and being taught certain things by Ananias was baptized Acts 9:5-18. So you see, it isn't the baptism that saves you, it's the baptism that shows that one has confessed a belief in the Lord Jesus Christ, the one who can and will save those who truly accepts him.

Baptism is symbolic of the death burial and resurrection of Jesus Christ. For true born again Christians, it's an outward show to the world of a person inward confession. Not all that are baptized are saved. Some that are baptized are just as lost when they come out of the water as they were before they went into the water. Romans 10:9-10 *says that if thou shalt confess with thy mouth the Lord Jesus, and shalt believe in thine heart that God hath raised Him from the dead, thou shalt be saved **(not is saved)**. For with the heart man believeth unto righteousness; and with the mouth confession is made unto salvation.* Just mere saying you believe with the mouth is not sufficient; one must truly believe with the heart. Mankind may believe your spoken words but God knows your heart and accepts only confessions of faith. Hebrews 4:12 says, *"for the word of God **is** quick, and powerful, and sharper than any two edged sword, piercing even to the dividing asunder of soul and spirit, and of the joints and marrow, and **is** a discerner of the thoughts and intents of the heart."*

After one has been baptized, he/she should then be taught how to live the Christian life. Satan knows at this point in one' life he/she is most vulnerable. Just as he tempted Jesus in Matthew 4:1-10, he will tempt each and every person that comes to Jesus. A new born Christian as a new born child must be taught what things are efficient and necessary for healthy physical and spiritual growth. If a new born baby is not watched and nourished by mature concerned adults, he/she will not receive the things sufficient for growth or life. In the same manner, mature and concerned Christian believers must teach and watch over newly born converts that they be aware of the proper way of serving God and his word. There's so much misconception about God word today; rarely do we hear it being taught for the purpose of saving souls. Few church goers even know how to serve God and don't even have any real concern about learning how. Our Christianity must supersede lip service and simply being hearers of the word. The scripture says it's the doers of the word that are justified not the hearers Romans 2:13 and James 1:22-23. But, in order to be doers of the word, one must know the word.

Baptism serves as a symbol of the washing away of our old life and conditions us for the new life in Christ Jesus. Baptism cannot cleanse the heart; repentance must be sought by the heart and confession must be made by the mouth Romans' 10. When the confession is real, the Lord Jesus accepts the confession and cleanses the heart of the confessor. It is the Lord that does the saving. Baptism is symbolic of Jesus' death burial and resurrection. It symbolizes the death of sin in our lives and the regeneration of a new life. It is a must for salvation and should be accepted willingly for all would be Christians. Baptism should never be forced upon any individual but should be offered and recommended to everyone that wishes to be saved. It is not the end of our Christian journey but the beginning. If leaders decline to supply new converts with the milk of the scriptures after they've been baptized, they will never grow nor learn the ways of the Lord.

It is a sad thing to say or do but it's true. There are many in leadership positions that do not want their people to know the truth. If the people knew the truth, many pretenders in leadership roles would be exposed for what they really are.

As long as evil seducers keep their congregations or other groups of people in the dark, they will continue to have the power to manipulate them. As I constant say to people, the scripture also confirms the same. As long as we have strength to walk out of darkness, we have a choice to do so at our will. The way out of spiritual darkness is within our midst but we have to want and accept that way. If we choose to stay in darkness, we condemn our own souls and that's our privilege to do so if we wish but when we choose to use our power to keep others in darkness, we have a greater punishment awaiting us in the judgment.

We read in the book of St. Matthew 18:6-8 " *but whoso shall offend one of these little ones which believe in me, it were better for him that a millstone were hanged about his neck, and **that** he were drowned in the depth of the sea. Woe unto the world because of offenses! For it must needs be that offenses come; but woe to that man by whom the offense cometh! Wherefore if thy hand or thy foot offend thee, cut them off, and cast **them** from thee: it is better for thee to enter into life halt or maimed, rather than having two hands or two feet to be cast into everlasting fire.*" To give up our own soul, is our choice but to cause others to lose their souls for our greed and self praises is a greater offense. It is better to live right with little and serve the Lord than to live unjust in the world with much.

What Is Communion And Should It Be Taken By Anyone Who Has Not Accepted The Lord Jesus Christ As His/Her Savior?

Answer: Communion is a sharing of the relationship between believers and Christ. It's a sacred service Christians share in with their Lord.

This relationship cannot be shared by unbelievers or by one whose life is burdened with sin without causing consequences. This religious sacrament is one in which unleavened bread and wine is partaken of in commemoration of the death of Jesus Christ. Only saved persons, after they've been taught the advantages and dangers of this sacrament, should partake or not partake of this service after careful examination being convinced in his/her heart that he/she is worthy or unworthy. To the righteous, communion represents a deeper understanding and relationship of their Lord; sharing in the Christian' communion service is a mean of bringing sickness and even death down on sinners and unbelievers.

Although, It is necessary for a person to partake of the Lord' body and blood in order to be saved, it is a dangerous thing to partake of it if you're unworthy." *Verily, verily, I say unto you, except ye eat the flesh of the Son of Man, and drink His blood, ye have no life in you. Whoso eateth My flesh, and drinketh My blood, hath eternal life; and I will raise him up at the last day. For My flesh is meat indeed, and My blood is drink indeed. He that eateth My flesh, and drinketh My blood, dwelleth in Me and I in him St. John 6:53-56.* Look also at 1 Corinthians 11:27-31. *Wherefore whosoever shall eat this bread, and drink **this** cup of the Lord, unworthily, shall be guilty of the body and blood of the Lord. But let a man examine himself, and so let him eat of **that** bread, and drink of **that** cup. For he that eateth and drinketh unworthily, eateth and drinketh damnation to himself, not discerning **(having or showing good judgment or understanding for)** the Lord's body. For this cause many **are** weak and sickly among you, and many sleep. For if we would judge ourselves, we should not be judged.* Keep in mind 2 Corinthians 13:5 that tells us to examine ourselves to determine whether we're in the faith or not. Not knowing can bring sickness and even death upon us unexpectedly. It will not be the Lord body that's harmed but one' own individual body. Everything and everybody involved with the communion table should be the subject of respect and honor.

Those that prepare and administer the communion for and to other members of the congregation should live an open example of a servant of God? All leaders should pattern their lives after Jesus Christ. A Leader should never ask those he/she leads to do anything they themselves are not doing or willing to do.

Unworthiness causes a greater punishment to be inflicted upon leaders than it does to others. "*My brethren, be not many masters, knowing that we shall receive the greater condemnation. For in many things we offend all. If any man offends not in word, the same **is** a perfect man, **and** able also to bridle the whole body James 3:1-2.*"

Though many people consider communion to be a simple ritual of plain unleavened bread and grape juice or wine (whichever one may feel comfortable using) that church people practice partaking of in their church services at various times of the week or month. At the forefront this may be all it is, but once it's prayed over, it becomes a sacred ordinance. The bread and wine is changed by the power of prayer and God to represent the body of our Lord and Savior Jesus Christ. Peter quotes Jesus as saying "be ye holy; for I am holy" (1 Peter 1:16). Since Jesus said he was holy and the bread and wine represent his body, we must consider it too to be holy. Therefore, those who partake of it and those who administer it to the people should be holy. The scripture says" "for what fellowship hath righteousness with unrighteousness?" And what communion hath light with darkness. And what concord hath Christ with Belial? Or what part hath he that believeth with an infidel? (2 Cor. 6:14a-15). The communion table is sacred and should never be taken lightly. Therefore, only those that has been selected and proven themselves to be God fearing men showing the presence of the Holy Spirit in their lives should prepare or serve the Lord' table. However, it is my belief that many that serve the Lord table are not aware of the need to be holy and honorable men. They have not been taught nor do they seem to understand the dangers of unworthiness surrounding their duty and service to God and the congregation they serve.

How Can I Understand And Believe A Book That Is Filled With Mysteries And Prophecies?

Answer: If we truly want to understand scripture, we can. We need only follow the advice of those God has inspired to teach us.

In the book of Hosea 3:6a God says *"My people are destroyed for lack of knowledge: because thou hast rejected knowledge."*
The words of Matthew 7:7-8 and Luke 11:9-10 are our starting point. *"Ask, and it shall be given you; seek, and ye shall find; knock, and it shall be open unto you: for everyone that asketh receiveth; and he that seeketh findeth; and to him that knocketh it shall be opened."*
We're further told by Jesus in St. John that all Christians **(those that believe on him)** who continues in his words shall know the truth of the scriptures mysteries removing doubts. Paul goes on in 2 Timothy 2:15 to say *"study to show thyself approved unto God, a workman that needeth not to be ashamed, rightly dividing the word of truth."*

When it comes to understanding the mysteries of the body' digestion system, we're ignorant yet it never worries or stops us from eating food because we're told and believe we need it in order to sustain our physical body and well beings. In the same manner, we're told and should understand that we need the bread of the scriptures in order to sustain our spiritual well beings that we may know the way to eternal life. Jesus is the way into the sheepfold **(eternal life).** There is no other way. St. John 14:6 declares that Jesus is the way, the truth, and the life: no man can come to God except they go through Jesus Christ (St. John Chapter 10). If our desire is to be saved, we must learn of him. Romans 10:14-15a reveals that one must be taught about Jesus and his word before one comes to believe. Belief must come by word of a preacher or true believer who has been sent by God. Everyone who says they've been called by God is not of God. We must learn to try the spirit by the spirit to see if they are of God. By a man' word he shall be justified or condemned. The fruit he/she produces will identify who he/she truly represent.

The Holy Spirit will make the word of God manifested. Jesus said the Comforter (which is the Holy Ghost) will teach us all things and bring all things **(things we have read, seen, or been taught)** to our remembrance St. John 14:26. Knowledge is available; we just need to read it and accept it. In Jesus, we can find and know the truth. The gift of the Holy Spirit reveals the mysteries and prophesies of scripture.

In Order To Serve God, Must One Give Up The Friends He/She Associated With Before Conversion?

Answer: If they're friends that lead a noticeable worldly life, it would be to your advantage to be careful where you go and what you engage in with them. Try to encourage them to become a child of God as you, if possible.

True friends would never stand in the way of your salvation. Instead, they would support your efforts to be saved even if they, themselves, do not want to be saved. A friend would never want to see any harm come to his/her friend. According to proverbs 17:17, a friend loves his/ her friend all the time. Solomon says *"a man **that hath** friends must show himself friendly: and there is a friend **that** sticketh closer than a brother Proverbs 18:24."* A trust worthy friend cannot be measured or matched. *"Ointment and perfume rejoice the heart: so doth the sweetness of a man's friend by hearty counsel Proverbs 27:9."*

A friend's wounds toward you are faithful. In other words, they'll tell you of your faults and short coming because they love you as God loves you and do not wish to see you lost. Their intentions are to chasten you to urge you back on the right track. The scriptures say God chasten those whom he loves Hebrews 12:6. In Proverbs 3:12 we read *'for whom the Lord loveth he correcteth; even as a father the son **in whom** he delighteth."* A friend that directs your attention to the wrongs you do, out of love and concern for your salvation, is a worthy friend to have.

One of the last commandments given by our Lord and Savior, Jesus Christ, was to love one another as he had loved us. Through our love for one another, the world will see that we belong to him. A person who speaks love without ever showing it is a hypocrite. A hypocrite shares no true love for self, God, or you. He/she is a pretender who hides behind reality by using words of deceitfulness to gain the favoritism of others. This is something that's becoming the norm among the church and government alike. In government for fear of losing a vote, men turns a deaf ear and blind eye to what they know is wrong. In the church, favoritism and one's own unfaithful life style prevent him/her from speaking out, avoiding touching on the truth.

Where Can I Find It In The Bible Where It Says Before The End Of Time You Won't Be Able To Tell One Season From The Other?

Answer: I've found no information to support such a scripture.

In the 24th Chapter of the book of St. Matthew, Jesus points out certain signs that shall appear before his second coming but points out that no one know when that final day will come. Yet the signs will appear as a warning to mankind that the end is drawing near. A soul that is not right with the Lord has an opportunity to get right as long as the blood still run warm in his/her veins. He also goes on to tell us a sign to look forward too before the arrival of summer. This sign he said would let us know that summer is near, not winter, fall or spring.

God created the seasons for man benefit. His promise to Noah after the flood was that *"while the earth remains, seedtime (spring) and harvest (fall), cold and heat, and summer and winter, and day and night shall never cease Genesis 8:22."* God is an unchanging God; this in Malachi 3:6, he declares. "For I **am** *the Lord, I change not; therefore ye sons of Jacob are not consumed."* Solomon was inspired by God in Ecclesiastes to write that there is a season to every purpose under the heaven. God is in control of nature and the seasons and he says the seasons shall continue in the order and purpose he intended them to be.

Daniel declares that wisdom and might belong to God for ever and ever and that God has the power to change time and seasons (Dan. 2:20-21). Though, God has the power to change the seasons, he has promised Noah that they shall continue for the purpose they were created for as long as the earth remains. We know that God does not and cannot lie; therefore the rumor of not being able to determine the seasons from one another must be one of Satan deceiving lies that has been passed down from mouth to mouth for generations. Although, we experience warm days in the winter and cool days in the summer sometimes, it does not confuse us, we still know the different between winter and summer and spring and fall.

Does The Bible Mention In Words That The Way To Salvation Is So Plain That A Fool Should Not Error In His/Her Efforts To Find It?

Answer: Again this seems to be another one of those paraphrase rumors that got started years ago and people are still quoting it as bible based. Although, there is a scripture that says *"and the parched ground shall become a pool, and the thirsty land springs of water: in the habitation of dragons, where each lay, **shall be** grass with reeds and rushes. And a highway shall be there, and a way and it shall be called The way of holiness; the unclean shall not pass over it; but it **shall be** for those: the wayfaring men, though fools, shall not err **therein Isaiah 35:7-8.**"*

Jesus said of himself I am the way, the truth and the life. He is the only true way to eternal life. He also said he was the door into the sheep fold. The way to salvation is plain and even the simplest person can understand that one must go through Jesus in order to get in. however, there is only one way to salvation and that way is through Jesus Christ. No thieves, robbers, nor fools, will by force or accidently stumble into the kingdom of God and Christ. God is truth; Jesus is truth and the only true way to eternal life. There're critics that say God watches over children and fools. In a sense, this is true. You see; God has a watchful eye over the entire world. It is not God' desire that any of us be loss that's why he sent his son to die for the sins of all mankind and offers the gift of eternal life to any and all that will accept it. Be aware; the way to Jesus is not only plain and simple; it's also fool proof.

Is There Any Scripture Where We Can Find Where Jesus Commissioned A Woman To Preach?

Answer: This is a good question. People over the years have used fragments of scripture to justify something they wanted to do and because few people ever read their bibles it makes it easier to convince others. This is a question everyone should decide for his/her self by making a thorough examination of the scripture. Let's go to scripture. The scripture clearly states, if a man desires to be a bishop, not a woman, not anyone who so desires but if a man desires to be a bishop, he, not she, must be. Read 1 Tim.3:1-7.

What is preaching? To preach means to deliver a sermon. A sermon is a discourse of religious instructions. To prophesy means to foretell future and past events, it may be done by men, women, boys, or girls. If simply speaking the word of God is preaching, Eve would be considered the first preacher Genesis 3: 2-3. There were a number of women prophetess but they were not commissioned to rule over men nor preach the gospel. They shared God word with men and supported them but never were they chosen to lead them. In fact there was a time where Aaron and Miriam spoke against Moses marriage of an Ethiopian woman, Miriam considered herself like Moses and Aaron as being spokesman for God. God called the three of them to the tabernacle of the congregation and said *"hear now my words: if there be a prophet among you, I the Lord will make myself known unto him**(not her)** in a vision, **and** will speak unto him **(not** *her) in a dream* Num. 12:6." For Miriam placing herself in a position unsanctioned by God, she **(not Aaron)** was punished with leprous and became white as snow. Read Numbers the 12th chapter. Whereas it is true Miriam was a prophetess (Exod.15:20), she was never said to be a leader of men or spokesperson for God. There were also other prophetess mentioned in the Old Testament as Deborah (Judges 4:4), Huldah (2 Kings 22:14), Noadiah (Neh.6:14) and an unknown prophetess mentioned in (Is.8:3) but none of these women were leaders or oversees of men. Men, however, in that ere did visit them to enquire if there were words from the Lord. There is no indication that these women carried the word of God from place to place as the men prophets did instead they seem to have shared the word from their homes or a stationary place. The same would seem to apply to the women that taught or inspired men in the New Testament.

In the New Testament we find a woman name Anna who was a prophetess in the temple when the baby Jesus was brought in Luke 2:36-38. The book of Acts tells us of the four daughters of Phillip, the Evangelist, that prophesied. These four daughters did prophesy **(teach)** and they did it in the house of their father. They were not call evangelists, prophets, preachers, pastors, or even deacons; the scriptures only said that they did prophesy. There's no mention of them prophesying anywhere else or being sent by God to preach. It is true some women were teachers and they did prophesy but it would seem they did it in the home or in private settings but not in the open congregation of the church. Consider Mary, the mother of Jesus, Elizabeth, the mother of John the Baptist, Lois and Eunice, the mother and grandmother of Timothy, Priscilla, one of Paul' helpers in Christ Jesus, Ruth, Esther, Rhoda,

Mary, the mother of John Mark, these women influenced many great men with their wisdom and they were great supporters of God' people, God' word, and God' service but I see no evident where God sent one to preach nor make the words spoken by Paul in 1Tim. 2:11-13, 1 Cor.14:33-35, Eph.5:22-24, annulled.

If we return to Genesis chapter two, we'll see where God made woman as a helper of and for man not an overseer or ruler. Man, according to Genesis three sixteen, shall rule over the woman. Man, according to Genesis 2:7, was created first; woman, according to Genesis 2: 22, was created later. Through the history of the scriptures, we see where the elder was usually respected as the head of the family or tribe. The curses of the serpent, woman, and man, found in Genesis 3:14-19 are still binding today. The serpent still crawls upon his belly eating dust; the woman still have pain in child birth; the man still has to work for his survival. As long as this earth stands, the curses are valid. 1 Cor.11:3 confirm the man to be the head of the woman as do 1Tim.2:9-15. God is the head of Christ yet he has put all things under his authority. However, it is understood that God, himself, is not and will never be under Christ' authority. It is God that set the order of things in creation. Peace could return to our land if we would just accept that order, respect it, and do our best to live by it. The whole duty of man is to fear God and keep his commandments Eccl.12:13.

Paul credited Lois and Eunice, Timothy' mother and grandmother, with the unfeigned faith found in young Timothy (2 Timothy1:5). This tribute is given to them for their faithful up- bringing of Timothy in the Lord. Paul said that the faith found in Timothy was first found in his grandmother and mother. It is obvious that they taught him from the age of a child in their home. And there was Priscilla, who helped her husband, Aquila, to expound unto Apollos the way of God more perfectly. She was a worshipper and servant of God that was equipped by God to help influence a man of God to grow to higher heights. Women were and are chosen by God for different tasks. Mary and Elizabeth were chosen to bare children that would and did change the way mankind serve the living God. Each woman' child was chosen for a different role; each woman supported the other and each woman fulfilled her role. Each woman had the gift of the Holy Spirit within them and each one did prophesy but neither was given the command to go out and prophesy or preach to the world.

After Jesus resurrection, Mary Magdalene and others came to the sepulcher seeking to anoint the body of Jesus. Prior to their arrival, Jesus had already risen. The women were told to go and tell Peter and the other ten disciples that they should go into Galilee and there they would see him. Critics would argue that Jesus sent the women to preach the first sermon but the scriptures don't say that Jesus sent these women to preach. He told them to go and tell his disciples where he would meet them; he did not tell them to go and tell the world. No commission was given to them to go and preach; they were told only to deliver a message to his disciples Mat.28:9-10, Mark 16:9-10, Luke24, John 20:1-18. I can find no solid evident anywhere where Jesus commissioned women to preach. However there is solid evident where men were commissioned to preach St. Mark 16:15-20, St. Matthew

28:16-20, St. Luke 24:45-49, St. John 20:21-23, Acts 1:4-8, Acts 5:19-21, Acts 8:26-40, Acts 9:4-16 just to name a few.

There were many women that aided Jesus in his ministry and there were many that aided Paul. Even today, without the support of women, many church doors would probably be closed. They play a very important part in the ministry. We should always keep in mind that Jesus is the head of the church and only he can add souls to the church. Men or women can add members to our local church roles but only God can add members to the heavenly church role. Our names being added to the local church role can obtain us a free spot in the local Cemetery but not eternal life.

In the book of Isaiah 55:8-11, we find these words. *For my thoughts **are** not your thoughts, neither **are** your ways My ways, saith the Lord. For as the heavens are higher than the earth, so are My ways higher than your ways, and My thoughts than your thoughts. For as the rain cometh down, and the snow from heaven, and returneth not thither, but watereth the earth, and maketh it bring forth and bud, that it may give seed to the sower, and bread to the eater: so shall My word be that goeth forth out of My mouth: it shall not return unto Me void, but it shall accomplish that which I please, and it shall prosper **in the thing** whereto I sent it.*

In 1 Timothy 2:11-15, Paul writes to Timothy. *Let the woman learn in silence **(quietly)** with all subjection **(submission)**. But I suffer **(permit)** not a woman to teach, nor to usurp **(exercise)** authority **(leadership)** over the man, but to be in silence.* Paul goes on in the next three verses to state his reason for making the previous statements. *For Adam was first formed **(created)**, then Eve.* All parents were born before their children and no matter how long a child lives he/she should never try to rule or boss their parents. Care for them in their old age, yes, boss them, no, verse 14, *and Adam was not deceived, but the woman being deceived was in the transgression **(sin).***

Returning to Genesis 3:14-15 we see the serpent punishment for his part in deceiving the woman was to eat dust and crawl upon his belly all the days of his life, He not only brought a curse upon himself but his seed also. In the 16th verse, the woman punishment is issued out. Her sorrows were multiplied and pains were to be added to her conception **(childbirth)** and her husband would rule over her. Like the serpent, the woman not only brought this burden upon herself but upon her seed as well. And thy desire **shall be** to thy husband, and he shall rule over thee. For man' part in the breaking of the law, the ground was cursed for his sake and man from that day forward would have to work for his living. As long as the man and woman were innocent, God protected them and provided for all their needs. Like a child, when he/she reaches the age of accountability or the age where they no longer wants to listen to their parents. Then, it's time for them to go out on their own and provide for themselves. These are God words and the New Testament indicates he never changed that order.

To the Corinthian church, Paul writes. *Be ye followers of me, even as I also **am** of Christ.* He says; as I am an example of Christ, ye be likewise and follow my example. (Verse 2) *now I praise **(commend)** you, brethren, that ye remember me in all things, and keep the* ordinances *(laws and decrees), as I delivered **them** to you. (Verse three) but I would have you know, that the head of every man is Christ; and the head of the woman **is** the man; and the head of Christ **is** God.* These verses co-in sides with what God said to Eve; he, **(the man)** shall rule over thee. I can find no justifiable evident to show where Jesus commissioned a woman to preach, to be a pastor, or evangelist but you decide for yourself.

However, Paul instructs Titus to set certain things in order in the church at Crete. Among those are the sacredness and duty of the aged women. In Titus 2:1-5, Paul says. *But speak thou the things which become sound doctrine: that the aged men be sober, grave, temperate, Sound in faith, in charity, in patience. The aged women likewise, that **they be** in behavior as becometh holiness, not false accusers, not given to much wine, teachers of good things; that they may teach the young women to be sober, to love their husbands, to love their children, **to be** discreet,(**capable of observing prudent silence**) chaste,(**pure in thought and act**) keepers at home, good,(**of a favorable character or tendency**) obedient to their own husbands,(**willing or inclined to obey**) that the word of God be not blasphemed.*

God, the creator of the heavens and earth and all there is, set things in the order and way he wanted them to be. We may not like many of his ways but he is God and he has the rights to do whatsoever he will. Like Satan, men and women have sought in many ways to be what God did not intend for them to be or do. The more mankind rejects God order of things it causes more of God wrath to be poured down upon the earth. Never before have I seen so many homes and cities destroyed by water, fire, storms, mud slides, and earthquakes. Diver diseases are popping up every year and violent is at an all-time high and getting worse every day. God said his ways and thoughts was not our ways and thoughts and we know his ways and thoughts are not only higher but superior to ours. If the lower species and plant life on earth can accept God order of thing, why can't man who is supposed to be of a higher learning? We each must stand before our judge one day to give an account of ours did' and didn't'. I can find no evident to support a woman being called to a role of Pastor, prophet, or deacon. If you are a woman and you decide to take on the role of church pastor, I urge you to thread very carefully and search the scriptures until you're convinced without a doubt that God is pleased with your decision. If God has chosen you, then do your best to fulfill his will but if not, to him you must answer and all that you sow, be it good or bad, right or wrong, you will also reap. The scripture in 1 John 3: 19-21 says "and hereby we know that we are of the truth, and shall assure our hearts before Him. For if our hearts condemn us, God is greater than our heart, and knoweth all things; beloved, if our heart condemn us not, **then** have we confidence toward God."

Does The Bible Say Money Is The Answer To All Things?

Answer: not really, the scripture says it in a different manner. Ecclesiastes 10:19a say *"a feast is made for laughter, and wine maketh merry: but money answereth all things. Keep in mind that the scripture also says the love of money is the root of all evil.*

It is true; money is a necessity of life but money has its limits. There is that possession that supersedes money. We read in Eccl. 7:12 the different between money and wisdom. *"For wisdom is a defense (asset), and money is a defense (asset): but the Excellency (best part) of knowledge is, that wisdom giveth life to them that have it.* Money can buy almost anything in this world but nothing in the kingdom of God and Christ. As money is a needful asset in life, it can also be a luring defect to life. In Acts 8:18-20, we read. *"And when Simon saw that through the laying on of the apostles' hands the Holy Spirit was given, he offered them money, saying, give me this power also, that anyone on whom I lay hands may receive the Holy Spirit. But Peter said to him, your money perish with you, because you thought that the gift of God could be purchased with money!" (New King James translation)*
Just because a person has money doesn't mean he/she is any better than anyone else. People with money feel they should be treated different and there're some people that cater to their belief. Money bought friend are not stationary; consider people who have had experiences with such friends as these, like the prodigal son in St. Luke 15:13-15.

The Apostle Paul tells young Timothy the danger of coveting **(unchristian like desires)** money. *"But godliness **(conforming to the laws and wishes of God)** with contentment **(peaceful satisfaction)** is great gain **(profit)**. For we brought nothing into this world, **and it is** certain we can carry nothing out. But they that will be rich fall into temptation and a snare **(trap)**, and **into** many foolish and hurtful lusts **(unrestrained cravings)**, which drown men in destruction **(ruin)** and perdition **(eternal damnation)**. For the love of money is the root of all evil: which while some coveted after, they have erred **(turned)** from the faith, and pierced themselves through with many sorrows. But thou, O man of God, flee these things; and follow after righteousness, godliness, faith, love, patience, meekness 1 Timothy 6:5-11."*

When money becomes the center of attention for religious or any other leaders, godly contentment becomes obsolete. In many of our churches today, money is a coveted commodity. The sins mentioned in Galatians 5: 19-21 that can cause one to be lost are rarely if ever mentioned. Some ministers are so wrapped up in their love for money they have forgotten their charge in 2 Timothy 4: Peter says to all leaders, *"feed the flock of God which is among you, taking the oversight **thereof,** not by constraint, **(constraint here seem to indicate that a person should not take over the leadership of God' flock by using the power of the office to force his congregation into doing anything. It also would seem to indicate that leaders should not hold back speaking the truth whether it reproves or corrects a person for his/her wrong doings or uplifts a person for his/her righteous deeds.)** but willingly **(voluntary, but one must also keep in mind that**

once he/she accepts the position, he/she becomes
responsible for everything surrounding that office.): not
for filthy lucre (money: Jesus asked the question, what
will a man give in exchange for his soul? Taking the
leadership role over God' people, one should be careful
not to be motivated by money or the lustful pleasures
and things surrounding money.), but of a ready mind
(Showing a passion for the good of those believers put in
his charge); neither as being lords (bosses or masters) over
God's heritage, but being examples (showing servant ship
through obedience to Christ) to the flock 1 Peter 5:2-3."

There is no harm in having money; there is no sin in
desiring money for spiritual or natural resources as long as
we're in control of the money and the money is not in
control of us. The love of money caused Judas to sell our
Lord. In the Parable of the rich Young Ruler of Mat.19:16-
22, it tells us the young ruler' heart and life was wrapped
up in what he had and he was not willing to give it up. In
Mat.16:26, Jesus asked. *For what is a man profited, if he*
shall gain the whole world, and lose his own soul? Or what
shall a man give in exchange for his soul. Will a person put
his/her salvation or natural life in jeopardy for the love of
money or the pleasures of this world? The rich young ruler
did. Judas did (Mat.26:15). Ananias and Sapphira did in
Acts 5:1-10. Eve did in Genesis 3:6. Achan did in Joshua
7:20-25 and others in our day and time have done the
same. Christian leaders and Christian people must be
careful not to allow money to be their primary concerns in
life. Money and other material wealth will cease someday
but our God who has the power of eternal life is eternal.
The almighty God or the almighty Dollar, we have the free
will to choose the one we place our allegiance too.

Can A Person Get A Religion?

Answer: Religion is not something you get; it is something you practice. It is something a person devotes his/her life to. It's a deep conviction of religious beliefs, practices, ordinances, and commitments. It requires faith, obedient, and control of one's feelings and desires demanding certain conditions and restrictions one must confirm to in order to maintain its sacredness. It is not something that is forced or should be forced upon a person but a belief that calls for obedient once it is freely entered into. Ordinances and commitments are required. In the case of the Christian religion, baptism, constant prayer, faithfully assembling together often, communion observance, repentance, love, a forgiving heart, but most of all obedient to God words and commandments are required.

Speaking on this subject, James 1: 26 says "*if any man among you seem to be religious, and bridleth* (**controls**) *not his tongue, but deceiveth his own heart, this man's religion is vain* (**worthless**)". In Matthew 15: 17-20a, Jesus said to Peter "*do not ye yet understand, that whatsoever entereth in at the mouth goeth into the belly, and is cast out into the draught? But those things which proceed out of the mouth come forth from the heart; and they defile the man. For out of the heart proceed evil thoughts, murders, adulteries, fornications, thefts, false witness, blasphemies; these are the things which defile* (**make unclean**) *a man*": So you see; it is a devoted profession that requires one to be faithful to its calling. Like any profession, if one's works, skills, or devotions, does not exemplify his/her character and duty, it taunts his/her efforts to influence others. James goes on in chapter one verse 27 to support this statement. He says; *pure religion and undefiled* **(faultless)** *before God and the Father is this, to visit the fatherless and widows in their affliction* **(distress, loneliness, unmanageable needs) and** *to keep himself unspotted* **(being taken- in or mixed up with the lusts and evils of the world)** *from the world.*

The Apostle does not mean you should do your sin under the cover of darkness. He's saying once you devote your life to God you should not do or get involved in anything that would cause a smear to your good name or limit your influence with others. If one's religion is real, it will be shown by his/her concern for widows and orphans in their times of need. His/her devotion will not only uplift the distressed heart but others will be encouraged by his/her devotion to duty. Watchful eyes are always focused upon the righteous. Whatever they do wherever they go, their character is viewed.

One's religion starts with one's mouth. Romans 10:9 tell us the steps to being saved start with the confession of the mouth. If the confession of belief truly comes from the righteousness in your heart, salvation is available for you. The words that come forth from the mouth can determine one's destiny. Of this, Mat. 12: 36-37 warns us. *"But I say unto you, that every idle word that men shall speak, they shall give account thereof in the Day of Judgment. For by thy words thou shalt be justified, and by thy words thou shalt be condemned".* If we're able to avoid causing offense by our words, we can maintain control of our tongue.

Proverbs 15: 1-2 gives us guidance when dealing with conflicts. It is when dealing with conflicts that we often let our guard down. *A soft answer turneth away wrath but grievous words stir up anger. The tongue of the wise useth knowledge aright: but the mouth of fools poureth out foolishness.* Anger is one thing that can cause disgrace to a person religion. Proverbs 21:23 says; *whoso keepeth his mouth and his tongue keepeth his soul from trouble.* When we're able to control our words, especially in times of anger, it avoids us from having later regrets. James 3:10 tells us blessings and cursing should not come from the same mouth. Religion is not and should not be a hidden disguise. It is an open confession shown through and in a person character and godly duty. It surrounds a set of rules and ordinances that the Christian life style is bound by. Can a person get a religion? A person can and must have one if he/she hopes to be saved. It is what identifies us as followers of Jesus Christ. Therefore, if a person has religion, his love and life style will be patterned after the example set by our Lord and Savior, Jesus Christ. The apostle James describes faith in James 2:14-20 by saying that true faith is demonstrated through works. In like manner, true religion is shown through our service to God and our fellowman, our character, and our devotion to the confession on which we have pledged our allegiance. If a person has the Christian religion, it will be visual. True religion cannot, should not, and will not, be hid.

Are All Sins Equal Or Some Greater Than Others?

Answer: though all sins are wrong, all sins are not equal. Some demand greater penalties than others.

All unrighteousness is sin: and there is a sin   not unto death 1 John 5:17. Verse 16 says *if any man sees his brother sin a sin* **which is** *not unto death, he shall ask, and he* **(God)** *shall give him* **(the one who has sinned)***life for them that sin not unto death. There is a sin unto death: I do not say that he shall pray for it.* Hebrew 6:4-6 further tells us *"for* **it is** *impossible for those who were once enlightened, and have tasted of the heavenly gift and were made partakers of the Holy ghost, and have tasted the good word of God, and the powers of the world to come, if they shall fall away, to renew them again unto repentance; seeing they crucify to themselves the Son of God afresh, and put* **him** *to an open shame"*. Judas Iscariot committed such a sin. He was chosen as one of the twelve and was given the power of the Holy Spirit to heal all manner of sickness and diseases and power against unclean spirits just as the other eleven were (Matthew 10:1-39). Peter declared in Acts1:17 and 25 that Judas was numbered with them and had obtained part of the same ministry as he and the other apostles but through his act of betrayal he lost his chance for eternal life.

Judas, himself, realized this in St. Matthew 27:3-5. *"Then Judas, which had betrayed him* **(Christ),** *when he saw that he was condemned,* **(he realized he had committed the unpardonable sin)** *repented himself,* **(he became sorrowful for what he had done but it was too** *late)* *and brought again the thirty pieces of silver to the chief priests and elders, saying, I have sinned in that I have betrayed the innocent blood. And they said, what **is that** to us? See thou **to that.** (as the chief priest felt no remorse for Judas, Satan and ungodly leaders have no remorse for the loss of our salvation. their only interest is fulfilling their selfish will and desires. it is up to each individual to make sure he/she is following the truth of God' word and not the sayings of men that are contrary to the word** *of* **God). And he (Judas) cast down the pieces of silver in the temple, and departed, and went and hanged himself.*

It is amazing how we only realize the full scope of our sins after they come to the light. While we're engaged in them, we never consider the magnitude of their hurt. As long as David thought his affair with Bathsheba was a secret, he was blind to the hurt he was causing but when it came to the light, he saw and reaped the result of it the rest of his life. Adam and Eve didn't realize the hurt of eating off the forbidden tree till they were able to see the result of their disobedient. Politicians, school teachers, police officers, and others, never see the hurt of their sins before they come to the light. The greater the sin, the greater the hurt, some sins we can repent of and eventually recover from but there is that sin in which one cannot recover from Heb.10:26.Which seems to point out that one can be on the road to salvation and willfully give it up on his own accord. There is a different between being on the road to salvation and being saved.

In St. John 10:19 Jesus tells Pilate, *"thou couldest have no power **at all** against me, except it were given thee from above: therefore he that delivered me unto thee hath the **greater sin".** Here he points out that the one who ignites the sin must reap a greater level of punishment than those who partake with the sin. The first books of the bible point out the various levels of sin and their atonement. Some sins carried the punishment of death while others carried a lesser punishment. Therefore the scripture points out that all sins are not equal but all sins are wrong and require repentance.

What Is The Whole Armor Of God?

Answer: it is what protects us from the evil desires and weaknesses of this world.

Eph.6:11-18 says *"put on the whole armor of God, that ye may be able to stand against the wiles **(cunning devices)** of the devil. For we wrestle **(struggle)** not against flesh and flood, **(a mortal)** but against principalities, against powers, against the rulers of the darkness of this world, against spiritual wickedness in high **places.** Wherefore take unto you the whole armor of God, that ye may be able to withstand **(resist temptation)** in the evil day, and having done all, to stand. Stand therefore, having your loins girt about with truth, **(having your priorities in tact with God' words and commandments)** and having on the breastplate of righteousness; **(the breastplate protect the most vulnerable part of the physical body. It indicates living a life before others that exemplifies a child of God).** And your feet shod with the preparation of the gospel of peace; above all, taking the shield of faith, wherewith ye shall be able to quench **(suppress)** all the fiery **(easily provoked)** darts **(sudden pains)** of the wicked. And take the helmet of salvation **(which is the Holy Spirit),** and the sword of Spirit **(the Christian weapon for fighting evil),** which is the word of God: praying always with all prayer and supplication in the Spirit, and watching thereunto with all perseverance and supplication for all saints;"*

The armor of God is not something we can just look in the closet and pull out at any time. It is not something someone else can give us. It is something we must earn through our connection with God and our faithful service to God and others. We need the whole armor of God to ward off the wiles of the devil but we must also know how to use that armor. To use it in the wrong manner does us more harm than good. With our armor, we must avoid showing respect of person. With our armor, we must show our faith through our works. With our armor, we must speak in a manner that is beneficial to all. Speaking in tongues are not recommended unless there is an interpreter. Speaking in an unknown tongue or using big words is not beneficial. 1Cor. 14: 8-13- *for if the trumpet give an uncertain sound, who shall prepare himself to the battle? So likewise ye, except ye utter by the tongue words easy to be understood, how shall it be known what is spoken? For ye shall speak into the air; there are, it may be, so many kinds of voices in the world, and none of them* **is** *without signification* **(meaning).** *Therefore if I know not the meaning of the voice, I shall be unto him that speaketh a barbarian* **(a primitive person),** *and he that speaketh* **shall be** *a barbarian* **(boor)** *unto me. Even so ye, forasmuch as ye are zealous* **(fervent)** *of spiritual* **gifts,** *seek that ye may excel to the edifying of the church. Therefore let him that speaketh in an* **unknown** *tongue pray that ye may interpret.* In verse nineteen, Paul said, *yet in the church I had rather speak five words with my understanding, that* **by my voice** *I might teach others also, than ten thousand words in an* **unknown** *tongue.*

When David went to battle the giant Goliath, Saul armed him with his own armor, put a helmet of brass upon his head and armed him with a coat of mail. As David girded his sword upon the armor that Saul had given him, he realized that he had not proved them **(he had no experience fighting with such weapons)** David realized that one cannot represent the living God with what other people have or knows. One must use the knowledge, faith, and ability, he/she has acquired through his/her self-experience in the service of the Lord. One should read 1 Sam. 17:34-51.

The evil day mentioned by the apostle Paul may come upon us at any time. Such a thing happened to Job when he lost his children and livestock but Job had the armor of God on and Satan' fiery darts **(the loss of his children, the loss of his flocks, the sickness to his body, the merciless attitude and faith of his wife, and the finger pointing criticism of his friends)** could not penetrate his shield of integrity. On his head he wore the helmet of salvation, this protected him when his wife said unto him Job 2:9, *dost thou still retain thine integrity **(uprightness)**? Curse God, and die. **(It would seem Job' wife should have been grieving with him since they both had loss the same thing, their children and their source of income. Although, she was not struck with sore boils as Job, she was his wife and she should have found a way to encourage and comfort him rather than speaking in a way that added more pains to what he was already feeling. Can you even imagine how Job must have felt hearing such words from one so close? Job' shield had to have been strong to withstand such hurtful words. Job answered his wife although his body was weak and decaying but his armor was strong).* Thou speakest as one of the foolish women speaketh. What? Shall we receive good at the hand of God, and shall we not receive evil (Job 2:10)?* In such a weak stage, his armor had to be strong to withstand the drilling from his closest friends who tried to convince him that his condition was a punishment for wrongs he had done (Job. 4-32). Job' breastplate **(lifestyle and character)** even had God bragging on him. His faith drove him to confess the words found in Job 1:21; *"naked came I out of my mother's* *womb, and naked shall I return thither **(back to the heart of mother earth): the Lord gave, and the Lord hath taken away; blessed be the name of the Lord".*** Job knew his creator, accepted, and trusted in his judgment.

When we're on our sick bed, we need the whole armor of God to keep us trusting in him without doubts. At the loss of loved ones, we need it for strength to keep us from questioning God. When severe trials and tribulations come upon us, it protects us from Satan wiles and gives us patience to wait on God' intervention in our lives. When our faith is challenged by others, the armor of God helps us keep our integrity during the conversation. The armor of God is needed to face each new day; without it, we're vulnerable to Satan' wits.

We further hear from Job in Job 3:25-26. *"For the thing which I greatly feared is come upon me, and that which I was afraid of is come unto me. I was not in safety, neither had I rest, neither was I quiet; yet trouble came".* From this passage, we're told by Job that trouble will come our way whether we want it or not no matter how careful or righteous we are. No parents expect or desire to bury their children; no man, woman, or child, wishes for a life of terminal illness yet these dark evils will touch all of our lives in some way. Every man, woman, and child, if they live long enough, will face an evil day or days in his/her life time. When that day comes upon him/her, he/she would do well to have God within his/her life. The evil day may be characterized by the loss of a loved one, the loss of a job, or the failure of one' health, loss of material or financial assets, tossed in the path of destruction, a state of fear or etc. Paul warns us of that pending day(s) and urges us to prepare ourselves that we might be able to stand.

Is There A Danger In A Christian Seeking To Be Financially Rich?

Answer: Yes there is.

Paul said in1 Timothy 6:7-11, *"for we brought nothing into this world, **and it is** certain we can carry nothing out. And having food and raiment, let us be therewith content. But they that will be rich fall into temptation and a snare, and **into** many foolish and hurtful lusts, which drown men in destruction and perdition. For the love of money is the root of all evil: which while some coveted after, they have erred from the faith, and pierced themselves through with many sorrows. But thou, O man of God, flee these things; and follow after righteousness, godliness, faith, love, patience, meekness"*.

Here we're told the dangers of wanting to be rich. It is a fact; the more we have the more we desire to have. The more we accumulate, whether it's money or material gains, the more we focus on trying to protect or up keep those gains. Unknowingly, if we are not extremely careful, our minds will shift from trying to please God to trying to secure a worldly life style.

A warning to the rich, the apostle James writes in Jas.5:1-6. *Go to now, ye rich men, weep and howl for your miseries that shall come upon you. Your riches are corrupted, and your garments are moth-eaten.*

Often ministers and others quote third John 1:2 and contrive it to God speaking to man but they're in error. It is not God speaking to mankind but the apostle

John speaking to his good friend. Let's go to scripture 3rd John 1-5. *The elder unto the well beloved Gaius, whom I love in the truth* (**this is John speaking not God**) *beloved, I wish above all things that thou mayest prosper and be in health, even as thy soul prospereth.* (**God does not have to wish that we prosper or be in health; he has the power to bless us with either or both at his will. Men on the other hand can only wish one another the best of health and good fortune.**) John, not God, goes on to say *for I rejoiced greatly, when the brethren came and testified of the truth that is in thee, even as thou walkest in the truth. I have no greater joy than to hear that my children walk in truth. Beloved, thou doest faithfully whatsoever thou doest to the brethren, and to strangers:* it is evident here that Gaius was one that had accepted the Lord Jesus under the leadership of the apostle John and had proven to be a very faithful servant. John here writes to him expressing his love and continuous desire for his physical and spiritual success. There's no indication to suggest that John was speaking of financial prosperity. One can prosper in various ways without becoming rich. When we consider what Jesus said concerning the difficulty of a rich man entering into heaven in Mat.19:23-24 and what Paul says in 1Tim. 6:19-11, it is very doubtful that an apostle of Jesus Christ would wish someone to be financially rich.

Being rich is not a sin. Many of the Old Testament Patriarchs were rich. Men like Abraham, Lots, Jacob, Isaac, Job, and Solomon, just to name a few, these men were faithful to God and never allowed what they had to come between them and their service to God. By the time the New Testament came in force, we see where richness had changed some men hearts toward evil, greed, and selfishness. Judas' greed for money caused him to betray his and our Lord and Savior Mt. 27:3-5. Simon, the sorcerer, thought to use money to finance his greed for popularity and praises Acts 8:5-24. Ananias and Sapphira' love of money and desire for human praises caused them to lie to the Holy Ghost, an evil that brought them immediate death Acts 5:1-10. The rich man we read about in St. Luke 16:20-31 richness made him too selfish to share what God had blessed him with to feed the hungry man Lazarus. In Mt. 19:16-23, we see where a young rich man chose his richness over eternal life.

Being rich can also serve a good and prosperous purpose. Jesus was rich yet he gave it up to come down to restore mankind back to God. The Good Samaritan used his richness to provide care for an unknown stranger's needs.

Although, I've heard it mentioned many times by Religious leaders and other church goers, I can find no scripture to support the saying that God want Christians to be financially rich. However, the scripture does point out that God wants us as Christians to be rich in love, good works, helps, and service to him and our' fellowman.

1 Tim.6:17-18 Paul said to Timothy, *charge them that are rich in this world, that they be not high-minded, nor trust in uncertain riches, but in the living God, who giveth us richly all things to enjoy; that they do good, that they be rich in good works, ready to distribute, willing to communicate.* James 2:5 tells us God has chosen the poor of this world rich in faith, to be heirs of the kingdom which he has promised to them that love him. Proverbs 22:1 point out that it is better to have a good name than great riches and loving favor than silver and gold. In fact, Jesus

tells us it will be hard for a rich man to enter the kingdom of heaven St Mark 10:23, Mt. 19:24, St. Luke. 18:25.

Since Jesus said himself it will be hard **(but not impossible)** for a rich man to enter the kingdom of heaven, why then would he say that God wants us all to be financially rich if it's going to have a bearing on us being saved. This would seem to be another of Satan' deceiving wiles. Paul said in 1 Tim 2:4 that God would have all men to be saved and come unto the knowledge of the truth? This scripture points out that it is God' will that all men be saved. So then why would he want us all to be rich if being rich can hinder our chance of getting into the kingdom of heaven? You hear some of the most prominent ministers declare over and over again that God wants us all to be financially rich but there's no scripture to back up their statement. They have developed a satanic altitude for greed. As Paul said to Timothy in 1 Tim.6, we must learn to be content with food and raiment and Jesus said that our heavenly father knows of all our basic needs

Being rich is many men and women desire. Their hearts linger for the pleasures the world has to offer. Like their unsaved counter parts, they crave exotic living, lavish vacations, pigging out at expense restaurants, and parading around in expense clothes and cars. Being rich up-lifts one' pride and causes one to focus on selfish wants more than on the living Lord who is the source of all our beings. Proverbs 10:15a says the rich man's wealth is his strong city. In fact, proverbs 23:4a tell us not to labor to be rich. God has promised to supply our needs; we need only trust him.

In Mat.6:19-21, we find these words. *Lay not up for yourselves treasures upon earth, where moth and rust doth corrupt, and where thieves break through and steal, but lay up for yourselves treasures in heaven, where neither moth nor rust doth corrupt, and where thieves do not break through nor steal: for where your treasure is, there will your heart be also.* Remember the rich man in St. Luke 12:16-22.

Many of us are rich and successful and don't even realize it. To have a roof over your head, clothes on your back, know where your next meal is coming from daily, and God on your side, you are rich above measure. Many poor people would give their right arm to have the pleasure of these things. God is provider for the righteous as long as they remain obedient to His commandments. He provided for Adam and Eve as long as they kept his commandment. He promised to take care of all of ancient Israel' needs once they entered the promise land as long as they remained faithful to His commandments.

Being rich will take nothing away from our character if we remain faithful to God. All of us have or will be taunted with the desire to become rich in this world. According to scripture, our desire to be rich can cause us to error away from eternal life. There's nothing wrong with wanting or having a large supply of almighty dollars as long as they don't draw our mind away from the almighty God. But we should always remember that in our efforts to attain the riches of this world it'll mean taking our focus off of God which can be a dangerous thing to do. The more time we put toward being rich, the less time we'll have to focus on God. The riches we gain through God' service we'll always have to cherish but the riches we gain of the world we'll someday have to leave behind.

Jesus said no servant can serve two masters; either he will hate the one, and love the other, or else he will hold to the one, and despise the other St. Luke 16:13a. To put it plainly, one cannot be a servant of God seeking spiritual riches being led by the spirit and one seeking worldly riches being influenced by the lust of the flesh. For Jesus says ye cannot serve God and mammon St. Luke 16:13b. Paul tells us in Romans 8:5 they that are after the flesh mind the things of the flesh and they that are after the spirit the things of the spirit. We must stop hiding behind the shield of ignorant. We cannot serve the best of both worlds though so many try too. Acting holy on Sunday then mixing in with the frolic of the world Monday through Saturday does not show the Christ within us but the deceitfulness of the devil. For what shall it profit a man if he shall gain the whole world, and lose his own soul? Or what shall a man give in exchange for his soul (St. Mark 8:36-37)? Is it worth a man holding on to the lusts of this world for a few days of pleasure on this side of the grave and lose eternal life on the other side of the grave?

Where Can I Find The Scripture That Says God Will Put No More On You Than You Can Bear?

Answer: Though people paraphrase the scripture in quoting it, there is such a scripture.

You'll find the actual scripture in 1 Cor.10:13. *There hath no temptation taken you but such as is common to man: but God **is** faithful, who will not suffer you to be tempted above that you are able; but will with the temptation also make a way to escape, that ye may be able to bear **it**.* This scripture tells us that any temptation that we're tempted with is a normal temptation that has been faced by others. It is good that we serve a God that is as wise as he is faithful. He knows just how strong each of us are therefore he will not allow the temptation to supersede our ability to bear it and with every temptation will make a way for us to endure or escape it. Once God provides the way out it will be up to us to take it. However, we should be careful not to take any situation for granted just because we have an advocate with the Father. If we have the strength to escape or avoid a sinful situation, we should do the right thing. David said in Psalms 19:12-13 *"who can understand **his** errors?" cleanse thou me from secret (unknown) **faults**. Keep back thy servant also from presumptuous **sins (sins we take liberties in doing)**; let them not have dominion **(rule)** over me: then shall I be upright, and I shall be innocent from the great transgression.*

We should be aware that there's a sin that can cost us our salvation. In Hebrew 10:26, we find these words. *For if we sin willfully after that we have received the knowledge of the truth, there remaineth no more sacrifice for sins, but a certain fearful looking for of judgment and fiery indignation, which shall devour the adversaries.*

No matter who we are, we'll face situations in life that places us between a rock and hard place. It may seem that our troubles are greater than anyone else' but every man, woman, boy, and girl will face things in life that make them feel they're all alone. I've learned from the scriptures and by listened to other individuals that we all have problems. Some problems we bring upon ourselves; some are caused by other people and things but we all have or will have them. With the help of the Lord, we can face and even overcome any and all problems that come our way. Some problems are brought upon us to test our faith and patience. One thing is for sure; it is better to face a problem with the Lord than to face one without Him. No problem is too large or small for the Lord to solve. The evils brought upon Job, God would not allow too come upon just any man. As the scripture points out, he knows how much each of us can bear. He knows us better than we know ourselves.

Whose Responsibility Is It To Visit The Sick And Shut-In?

Answer: it is every Christian' responsibility but leaders as Jesus did should set the example.

Some leaders will tell you it's the Deacons job to visit the sick and shut- in not the pastor or minister. However, this is not what the scripture teaches. In the book of James chapter 1:25-27 we see how pure religion is defined. *But whoso looketh into the perfect law of liberty, and continueth **therein**, he being not a forgetful hearer, but a doer of the **Work**, this man shall be blessed in his deed. If any man among you seems to be religious, and bridleth not his tongue, but deceiveth his own heart, this man's religion **is** vain. Pure religion and undefiled **(unpolluted or corrupted, without fault)** before God and the Father is this, to visit the fatherless and widows in their affliction, **and** to keep himself unspotted from the world.*

Every person that professes to be a child of God has a duty to visit the sick if his or her conversion is true. Pastors and others church leaders should take the lead role. Look at James 5:13-15. *Is any among you afflicted? Let him pray. Is any merry? Let him sing psalms. Is any sick among you? Let him call for the elders of the church; and let them pray over him, anointing him with oil in the name of the Lord: and the prayer of faith shall save the sick, and the Lord shall raise him up; and if he have committed sins, they shall be forgiven him.*

You see where the scripture said let the sick call for the elders of the church? Who are the elders of the church? Are pastors considered in this list or is it specifically talking to the Deacons or some other group? Let's look at a few scriptures and see who are considered as elders. 1 Peter 5:1-4 *the elders which are among you I exhort(), who am also an elder,* **(here we see Peter confess himself to be an elder)** *and a witness of the sufferings of Christ, and also a partaker of the glory that shall be revealed: feed the flock of God which is among you, taking the oversight* **thereof,** *not by constraint***(compulsion),** *but willingly; not for filthy lucre* **(sordid gain),** *but of a ready mind* **(willing mind);** *neither as being lords over* **God's** *heritage, but being examples to the flock.* In 3 John1:1, John identifies himself as being an elder. Paul also considered himself as an elder. In Philemon 1:9, he referred to himself as Paul, The aged.

Peter called for the elders **(pastors)** to feed the flock of God in which they had been made overseers of and urged them to be an example to the flock in which they led. As Jesus showed himself an example to his disciples **(who later became apostles)** St. John 13:13-15 *ye call Me Master and Lord: and ye say well; for* **so** *I am. If I then,* **your** *Lord and Master, have washed your feet; ye also ought to wash one another's feet. For I have given you an example, that ye should do as I have done to you.* When Lazarus was sick, his sisters sent for Jesus John 11:1-7. When Jairus' daughter was sick St. Marks 5:22-24, who did Jairus send for? When a centurion's servant was sick St. Mat.8:5-13, who did the centurion' seek? In each of these cases, Jesus was sought and he went without question to serve the need of the sick. Jesus, the chief shepherd, set the example for all under shepherds to follow. Paul said in 1 Cor.11:1*"Be ye followers of me, even as I also* **am** *of Christ."* He further states in Phil.3:14-17, *I press toward the* *mark for the prize of the high calling of God in Christ Jesus, let us therefore, as many as be perfect, be thus minded: and if anything ye be otherwise minded, God shall reveal even this unto you. Nevertheless, whereto we have already attained, let us walk by the same rule. Let us mind the same thing. Brethren, be followers together of me, and mark them which walk so as ye have us for an example.* Jesus took the time to administer to the sick and needy without complaining or dreadfulness even when he was tired and hungry St. John 4:1-34.

Often leaders today complain about what they do and how tired they get when they're confronted about the visitation of the sick. Either they make excuses or will tell you it's the job of someone else to visit the sick. Before accepting the leadership over a church congregation, one should look into what God requires and expects. Since it is a position of desire accepted by one' free will, according to1Timothy3:1, once accepted accountability is required. Excuses are not. Remember the calling of Moses by God; Moses made excuses of his weaknesses but God reminded him of who made man and everything about man' physical condition Exodus 4:1-12. When one feels weakness in performing the role of leadership, one should consider the words of Isaiah 40:28-31. *Hast thou not known? Hast thou not heard **that** the everlasting God, the Lord, the Creator of the ends of the earth, fainteth not, neither is weary? **There is** no searching of his understanding. He giveth power to the faint; and to **them that have** no might he increaseth strength. Even the youths shall faint and be weary, and the young men shall utterly fall: but they that wait upon the Lord shall renew **their** strength; they shall mount up wings as eagles; they shall run, and not be weary; **and** they shall walk, and not faint.*

Let's return to James 5:14-15. Is any sick among you? Let him call for the elders of the church; and let THEM **(notice, he said, let them; here it would indicate he is saying in caring for the needs of the sick members of the church, the elders of the church should go as a group or with a group and pray in unity. One person cannot represent the church. The church is defined as a group of baptized believers in Christ. One person is not the church. This is not to say that the entire congregation should go. Jesus said in Mat. 18:20** *"for where two or three are gathered together in my name, there am I in the midst of them."* **there is strength in unity. The Psalmist said in Psalm 133:1,** *"Behold, how good and how pleasant it is for brethren to dwell together in unity!"* **We can see the strength and power of prayer in unity when Peter was imprisoned by Herod. The church without ceasing made prayer unto God for him. God heard and answered their prayer and freed Peter from bondage Acts12:1-12)** pray over him, anointing him with oil in the name of the Lord: and the prayer of faith shall save the sick, and the Lord shall raise him up; and if he has committed sins, they shall be forgiven him. James points out here that it is the elders **(ministers)** of the church that should go and administer the prayer of faith in unity and through their prayer of unity and faith the sick not only will be healed but if any sins have been committed by the person who is sick they too shall be forgiven.

Anointing is an authority and right of God. In the Old Testament, God commissioned certain prophets and certain priests to anoint special people and things for specific purposes. Jesus commissioned the twelve to preach, heal, and cast out devils in St. Mark 6:12-13. *And they went out, and preached that men should repent. And they cast out many devils, and anointed with oil many that were sick, and healed them.* The scriptures, both Old and New Testaments, show anointing only being done by God, Jesus, or those in leadership positions but never by lay persons or others for healing or office of authority.

This is not to say that every child of God should not visit one another when they're sick, lonely, heavy burdened, or simply for reasons of fellowship. It is saying that regarding the sick leadership has a responsibility and each individual person has a responsibility Mt. 25:34-40. We should always remember the golden rule. *Therefore all things whatsoever ye would that men should do to you, do ye even so to them: for this is the law and the prophets Mt.7:12.* If we're sick, we like to know that other people are concerned about our wellbeing and feelings. We should feel the same way toward our fellowman. It is every Christian duty to pray for one another. However, in all things, leadership should take the lead role and teach others to follow their examples. Leaders should follow Jesus example and avoid men examples. Jesus in speaking of the leaders of God' people when he was on earth said in St. Mat. 23:2-4 *"The scribes and the Pharisees sit in Moses' seat: **(as leaders of God' people)** all therefore whatsoever they bid you observe, **that** observe and do; but do not ye after their works: for they say, and do not. For they bind heavy burdens and grievous to be borne and lay **them** on men's shoulders; but they, **themselves** will not move them with one of their fingers:* many leaders have no problem pointing out what others should do or be doing but make excuses when they're questioned concerning their failure to act. Never ask others to do what you are not willing to do yourself. A great leader demonstrates in deeds the things he/she teaches others to do.

Who Was Or Is Melchizedek?

Answer: Melchizedek or Melchisedec was the priest of the Most High God and king of Salem.

The first mention of Melchizedek is found in Genesis 14: 17-18." *And the king of Sodom went out to meet him (**Abraham**) after his return from the slaughter of Chedorlaomer, and of the kings that **were** with him, at the valley of Shaveh, which **is** the king's dale. And Melchizedek king of Salem brought forth bread and wine: and he (**Melchizedek**) **was** the priest of the Most High God.* Here we see that this Melchizedek was both a king and priest. This was an unusual double for any man to be. David and Solomon were considered to be king and prophet; Eli held the office of priest and judge, Samuel held the office of judge and prophet but only Melchizedek and Jesus is referred to as king and priest. Not just king and priest but kings of righteousness and peace and priests of the Most High God. Not a priest made by earthly men to oversee their religious affairs but they were priests of the eternal God.

When we go to Hebrews 7: 1-4, we see more insight into the life of Melchizedek. *For this Melchizedek, king of Salem, priest of the most high God, who met Abraham returning from the slaughter of the kings, and blessed him; to whom also Abraham gave a tenth part of all; first being by interpretation king of righteousness, and after that also King of Salem,(**Salem is the name for Jerusalem**) which is, king of peace; without father, without mother, without descent (**lineage or ancestry**), having neither beginning of days, nor end of life; **it is not clear**

what the writer is referring to here. It may be he is saying there is nothing known about his birth or death. The truth is there is not enough information concerning Melchizedek to draw a conclusion to his identity) *but made like unto the Son of God (****this tell us his appointment was by God as was Christ; neither was of the blood line of Aaron and both preceded Aaron' birth****) abideth* **(Remains)** *a priest continually (***indefinitely without interruption)**.Christ' priesthood shall have no ending.

Now consider how great this man **was***, unto whom even the patriarch Abraham gave the tenth of the spoils.* The fact that he is referred to as a man indicates that he was real. We also see that like Christ he was also righteous and a man of peace. The only man in scripture compared to the Son of God. verse 5 goes on to say *"And verily they that are of the sons of Levi, who receive the office of the priesthood, have a commandment to take tithes of the people according to the law, that is, of their brethren, though they come out of the loins of Abraham: but he* **(Mechisedec)** *whose descent* **(genealogy)** *is not counted* **(descended)** *from them* **(the sons of Levi)** *received tithes of Abraham, and blessed him that had the promises.* Those priests that followed the order of the Leviticus priesthood received tithes from the people but this priest, Melchizedek, who was not of the blood line of Aaron, yet he was a priest, received tithes from Abraham preceding the law. Abraham gave tithes to Melchizedek not by force of the law but freely by choice.

Do The Scriptures Say We Should Forgive Others Of Their Trespasses Against Us And Forget The Deed That They Did Against Us As Well?

Answer: though the scriptures say we should forgive one another, it does not however tell us we should forget. Although we should pardon a person and not hold the sin against them, forgetfulness will not be as easy to achieve.

In the model prayer that Jesus left on record, it states in (St. Mt. 6:11-12 and 14-15) *"and forgive us our debts, as we forgive our debtors"*. When we pray these words to God, we're asking him to forgive us in the same manner or way we forgive our fellow man. He further says in verse 14 through 15, *"for if ye forgive men their trespasses your heavenly Father will also forgive you: but if ye forgive not men their trespasses, neither will your Father forgive you"*.

We've all done something wrong or mistreated someone within our life time that we're not proud of. Whether we went to those people and asked forgiveness or not will not erase our memories of those incidents. As Christians, when we do wrong, we must first acknowledge to ourselves we've done wrong then repent by becoming bodily sorrow and go to the person(s) we've wronged and ask forgiveness. After we've sought the person(s) forgiveness, we must proceed to ask God' forgiveness: when we've done wrong, although we want forgiveness, we should never hope or think that the incident will easily be forgotten. The scriptures tell us that we sow we shall also reap. It is hypocritical for us to think other people should forgive and forget the wrongs we do to them when we never forget the ones we do to them.

Let's consider the words forget and forgiveness. Forget means to never be able to recall an incident again; whereas forgiveness means to pardon, free or excuse one from the penalty surrounding a fault. Forgiveness also means once we've forgiven one for his/her sin(s) we will not hold or use that sin against the person any more. In accordance with the Christian' religion, when we truly repent of an incident done to mankind or God, the incident can no longer effect our chance for eternal life; Though, the incident will be forgiven, it may not be for gotten. It will largely depend on the severity of the sin. When we were children, our parents punished us when we did wrong. The method of punishment they used showed us the penalty for doing wrong and it was a constant reminder of how wrongs hurt. They did it because they loved us and did not want to see us go astray. As mature Christian, we've learned from scripture that God chasten those he loves. In other words, he has a way of returning the wrongs we've done back upon us to haunt us for our actions, whether performed or neglected. To put it plainly, the things we sow, we will someday, somehow, also reap.

Romans 3:23**(the scripture that so many ministers and would be Christians hide behind to justify their wrongs instead of admitting and asking for forgiveness for their mistakes)** says *"for all have sinned, and come short of the glory of God"*. If we read Galatians 3:22, we'll see that the scripture hath concluded all under sin, that the promise by faith of Jesus Christ might be given to them that believe. This includes every human being on earth whether dead or alive. This is why Romans 3:23 says all have sinned and come short of the glory of God but this scripture does not give us a license to continue sinning and making excuses for our wrong doings. It says all have sinned not all are.

If leaders are hypocritical, they'll be poor examples for their flock to follow to the risen Lord. 1 Peter 4:17-18 says *"for the time **is come** that judgment must begin at the house of God: and if **it** first **begins** at us (church people), what shall the end **be** of them that obey not the gospel of God? And if the righteous scarcely be saved, where shall the ungodly and the sinner appear"?* Peter goes on to say in 2 Peter 2:21 concerning false preachers and teachers who know the truth but fail to live up to it *"for it had been better for them not to have known the way of righteousness, than, after they have known **it** to turn from the holy commandment delivered unto them".* We place too much emphasis upon Romans 3:23 and not enough upon Romans 6:23. God is a forgiving God but he never forgets his words and promises. The soul that sin shall die but if we confess our sins he will forgive us and restore us back into the fold.

Everyone has a past; some people prefer forgetting their past but the past plays an important role in what we are today. There's some good and some bad in each of our past. We would probably like to forget the past but it is as much a part of us as the present. When we think of where we came from and consider where we are today, as Christians, we realize it was God that brought us thus far. If we were to forget the past, we might forget who brought us to where we are today.

God instructed ancient Israel to build reminders to remind them and their children of the evils they faced in the past as well as the deliverances. The Israelites bondage in Egypt is still taught and preached today. The evils of Sodom and Gomorrah are still remembered. The sin of Cain, of Judas, of David, Solomon, Achan, Ananias and Sapphira, even as far back as Adam and Eve the sins committed are still remembered. We remember them and we learn from them. Like our personal sins, we can ask and be forgiven of them but from time to time their remembrance will enter our minds. The Old and New Testaments speak of forgiveness many times but not so much of forgetfulness. It is a strange thing that some people want others to forgive and forget the faults they commit but refuse to return the favor when the tables are turned. By remembering our faults, we can measure our growth and decline.

What Is The Difference Between Solomon's Evil Days Mentioned In Ecclesiastes 12: 1-8 And Paul's Evil Day Mentioned In Ephesians 6: 10-18?

Answer: Solomon' evil days is referring to old age but Paul' evil day is more or less referring to a tragedy that may arrive any day or at any given moment.

In Ecclesiastes 12:1-8, Solomon begins by saying, *"remember now thy Creator in the days of thy youth, while the evil days come not, nor the years draw nigh, when thou shalt say, I have no pleasure in them; while the sun, or the light, or the moon, or the stars, be not darkened, nor the clouds return after the rain:* **Here Solomon, the wisest man that ever lived, tells us while we're young we should acknowledge the Lord and his ways in the days of our youth before the dark days of old age approach. We should take pleasure in serving the Lord while we still have the full use of all our members, the hands, feet, eyes, ears, mouth, and mind. While we're young we're full of Energy, able to move about without tiring, great eye sights, great strength in our limbs, keen hearing ability, and great reasoning ability. Youth should not only have the urge to serve; they also have the Entergy to serve. In our youth, we can do a whole day' work and never get tired but when we reach our latter days a whole day' work or a night or day of pleasure will drain us of all our energy. The clouds return after the rain.**
.

Let's continue with verse three. *In the day when the keepers of the house shall tremble, and the strong men*

*shall bow themselves, and the grinders cease because they
are few, and those that look out of the windows be
darkened, and the doors shall be shut in the streets, when
the sound of the grinding is low, and he shall rise up at the
voice of the bird, and all the daughters of music shall be
brought low;* if the house is represented as the body,
then the keepers of the house refer to the hands and
arms. We use the hands and arms to feed the body,
clothe the body, protect the body, and to provide for
other needs of the body. When we're young they're two
of the most powerful members of our body, but as we
grow older, they become weak and begin to shake and
tremble. The strong men bow down this must have
reference to the legs. The legs of the young are strong
and able to carry the weight of the body without faltering
even when one is carrying a load but as we grow older
the legs become weak and feeble forcing the knees to
bend under pressure. The aged many times need the help
of a cane or walker to support the body in getting
around. Getting in and out of cars becomes difficult; long
walks and standing become painful. The strong men of
youth that are able to carry their own load must depend
on the support of others when they become aged. The
grinders are the teeth. When we're young, we have all
thirty-two of them and they're strong. We're able to eat
the foods of our choice without hesitation. As we grow
older we start losing our teeth and the ones that are left
becomes weaker, we'll come to realize we can no longer
eat the foods we once ate as a result of few, weak, or no
teeth. Those that look out of the windows be darkened is
referring to the dimness of the eyes. As one age, one's
eye sight falters; one cannot see as far or good as he/she
once did. I can remember when I could see the smallest
print on a coin now I need glasses with the support of a

magnifying glass to see those small prints. In my days of youth, I could look far across the land and recognize who a person was by the person way of movement. As I continue to age, it may become difficult for me to recognize a person standing at my own front door.

I remember visiting a lady who knew me well but as I knocked at her door with only a glass door between us she was still unable to recognize me. She was an evangelist but old age had come upon her and the light of the sun, moon, stars, and light were darkened. When we see these things happening to others, we have an idea of what awaits us in our future.

Verse four says and the doors shall be shut in the streets, when the sound of the grinding is low, and he shall rise up at the voice of the bird, and all the daughters of music shall be brought low; and the doors shall be shut in the streets. This no doubt refers to the lips and jaws. As youths, if we're not flattering the lips telling something, we're questioning someone to learn something. When we're young, it seems everybody wants our advice but as we grow older and older people seem to shun our advice. The elderly talks more to themselves than they do to others. Old age is the loneliest stage of a person life. Many times the aged feels shut out from the rest of the world. "and the sound of grinding is low" this is a picture of old age when eating soft foods make little or no sound because we're toothless or with crowns. "And all the daughters of music shall be brought low" This verse deals with the loss of our hearing ability. . Sounds will become weaker and weaker with age. When I was a child, I slept through storms and other loud noises but now in my old age I rise up like the early bird. Pains are with me when I go to bed; pains are with me when I get out of bed in the morning. I sometimes watch my grandchildren sleep from morning to evening and I stare at them wondering how they do it. It is a good thing to be in the Lord when we reach old age. Because of our aches and pains, our constant need for rest, organ failures, and other body weaknesses, we need the Lord to give us strength to face the trials of each new day. And all of the daughters of music shall be brought low. The strong deep voice we once had will fail to be as loud or entertaining as it once was. The ears will cease to hear clearly the sweet sounds they once heard. Even the joyful sounds of the wind, rain, birds, trees, and other creatures of nature will become hard for us in our old age to hear.

Verse five begins with the fear that invades the mind as one grows older. *Also **when** they shall be afraid of **that which is** high, and fears **shall be** in the way, and the almond tree shall flourish, and the grasshopper shall be a burden, and desire shall fail: because man goeth to his long home, and the mourners go about the streets:* **when I was young, me and my siblings would climb the highest trees for fun; climb upon house tops and jump off time after time like it was a game; heights were no problem to climb or jump and we faced dangers with a smile. Now that I've grown older, I hesitate to climb a ladder; a two feet high fence I have doubts of clearing; and a two feet wide ditch I question myself whether I can jump over it or not. I am terribly fearful of heights and I sense danger in nearly every move I make. Jumping and skipping like the grasshopper in my youth was fun. Someday, the same limbs I used to have fun with will become feeble, weaker, and unbearable to get around on. They could become a burden to travel on even with the use of a** cane. The almond tree is the head. As we grow older, the hairs on the head turn whiter and whiter till there is none. Some people say a white head is a sign of wisdom and so it is. It's a sign of wisdom that tell us we can no longer do the things we use to do without causing hurt to our body and health. As youths, we worked in the fields and often in our spare times we observed and played like the grasshopper, old age puts a stop to that bouncing around. Every step I now make sends a pain throughout my body. Loud noises and children crying or playing get on my nerves. Things that once were a joy now are annoying. Sexual pleasures of youth fade out when one grows older. When life becomes more of a burden than pleasure and pains become unbearable, death is the next most joyful thing that man has to look forward to. As man grows older, he begins to wonder about what mourners will say about him at his death. Some will even make out their obituary before their death in an effort to make sure good things are said about them when they're gone.

Verse six focuses our attentions on the break downs of the body as we grow older. *Or ever the silver cord be loosed, or the golden bowl be broken, or the pitcher be broken at the fountain, or the wheel broken at the cistern.* The sixth verse urges us to serve the Lord before the organ start breaking down or growing weak. The silver cord may refer to the spinal cord, the golden bowl the head, the place where the brain is located. Youth enjoys an age where their thinking and reasoning abilities are at their peak. Those abilities start decreasing in efficiency as we reach old age and continues to lessen as we grow older and older. The pitcher be broken at the fountain could be referring to a failing heart. A pitcher is used to hold liquid but if the pitcher cracks it will become useless. The heart pumps blood throughout the body. If it falters, death comes into play. The wheel can be referred to as the system of veins and arteries stretching to and from the heart or even the lungs. An automobile cannot move without the use of the wheels. Without the ability to breathe on our own, we cannot move. We'll either be bed ridden or confined to a wheel chair. Even though the heart and other organs can be replaced, replacements can never restore the full function of the original body parts. With replacement parts, there are always restrictions. These parts are needed for life to continue and every time one fails one's ability to serve becomes compromised but as we grow older we can expect these parts to fail or weaken one after the other.

Now, we come to verse seven, the end of life. *Then shall the dust return to the earth as it was: and the spirit shall return unto god who gave it.* Man is flesh made out of dust. Genesis 2:7 says *"and the Lord God formed man of the dust of the ground, and breathed into his nostrils the breath of life; and man became a living soul."* This tells us man was formed (or made) from the dust of the earth. Man was molded into form from dust but he was only a figure made out of dirt before God breathed the breath of life into him. Without the breath of God, man was only a pile of erected dirt. It took the breath of God to make man a living soul. Though man is a living soul, he owes his existence to the earth and God. His flesh belongs to the earth; his spirit belongs to God. At death, the flesh (which is made out of dust) will return to the earth where it came from and his spirit (which is the breath of life) will return to God who gave it.

Finally, we come to verse eight. *Vanity of vanity, saith the preacher; all **is** vanity.* Vanity is defined as emptiness and futility. Man' success or hope in life is and will be worthless and hopeless without God. David says in the 39th Psalm that every man at his best state is altogether vanity. Jesus points out in John15 that he is the link to man survival. Even from the beginning, we see it took the breath of God to make man a living soul. Our dependence does and always will depend on the Lord. If a man lives his life as he pleases, it will only bring him grief and distress down the road. Be not deceived; God is not mocked: for whatsoever a man soweth, that shall he also reap. For he that soweth to the flesh shall of the flesh reap corruption; but he that soweth to the Spirit shall of the Spirit reap life everlasting (Galatians 6:7-8).

Summary to Ecclesiastes 12:1-8

Returning back to Ecclesiastes 12:1 where the writer says "remember now thy creator in the days of thy youth", we get a better understanding of this statement when we reach our advance old age or when we associate ourselves with the very aged. In St. John 21:18, Jesus gave Peter insight of what to expect when he reaches his old age. Reminding him how he had the ability to dress himself and strength to walk without being led while he was young but the time would come when he would have to depend on someone else to dress and lead him around.

At the present, I'm well into my sixtie s and for a number of years I've noticed a decline in my body ability to function as it did in the days of my youth. My arms are not as strong as they once were; many times I notice my hands shake and tremble when I'm holding on to things. I'm unable to lift the amount of weight I once lifted with my arms and they constantly ache with arthritic. The ability to run and jump as fast and high with my legs I can no longer do. My eye sight has grown weaker; even with the use of eye glasses I cannot see as good as I did in my youth. My hearing has grown dim so understanding others speech is sometimes difficult and my mind is not as sharp as it once was. Though I still have the desire and ability to serve God and others, having less energy, it is not as easy as it was in my youth. Acknowledging this, I realize why Solomon says remember **(rather he says serve)** thy Creator in the days of thy youth. The older we become the harder it will be for us to use our limbs and mind in service. Of course if we're brought up in the Lord, we'll have the desire but not the ability to serve. Apart from what Solomon says, my fore parents had a saying about people that waited until they got well up in age before they started thinking about the Lord. They'd lived for pleasure the majority of their lives; then with, according to my fore parents, one foot in the grave and one on a bananas peel, they wanted to serve the Lord but their usefulness had declined.

Recently my father, who is ninety-five years old, broke his left hip and had to go through weeks of therapy to regain the ability of his leg to function again on its own. Visit after visit, as I visited him, I saw the fulfillment of Solomon' words. Each visit, I saw more of what Solomon was saying about the latter end of old age. The strength of his arms had grown so weak he found it difficult to open the top of a water bottle. Trying to open a flip phone frustrated him; he needed ear plugs in order to hear and even they sometime irritated him. Getting in and out of the bathroom aggravated him. He needed oxygen to help with his breathing and blood thinners to keep his blood from clogging. With little ability to serve himself, he was forced to depend upon others for sufficient care.

Now I sometimes set and wonder is this the fate that awaits me in the near future. Already I'm feeling some of the symptoms. Less than two decades ago I was visiting eight to nine homes each week praying or talking to those who were sick or elderly but today just visiting two or three homes wears me out. It's a great satisfaction knowing from my youth my mother taught me and all my siblings the ways that God would have us to go. Because of the way she brought us up, there are many things we'll not have to worry being questioned about in the judgment.

Every Christian desire is to be saved and to lead others to the one that has saved them. As Christians, we have a duty and responsibility to live a righteous life before God and our fellow man. In Ecclesiastes 11:9-10, the writer says *"rejoice, o young man, in thy youth; and let thy heart cheer thee in the days of thy youth, and walk in the ways of thine heart, and in the sight of thine eyes: but know thou, that for all these **things** God will bring thee into judgment. Therefore remove sorrow from thy heart, and put away evil from thy flesh: for childhood and youth **are** vanity.* God created us with a free will and allows us to live life as we please. But Solomon warns us of the fact that even though we have the free will to live as we please, there's a penalty for ungodly living.

Haiku Expressing The Poetic Circumstances Surrounding The Aged:

Haiku is a seventeen syllable poem. It is composed of three lines. The first line of five syllables: the second line of seven: and the third line of five (5-7-5): many haikus carry a hidden agenda others may be viewed as a riddle yet others may be pure poetic.

I started on four
Later, I stood up on two
Now I walk with three

With soup and jell-Lo
Nourishment will still resolve
When the grinders cease

Bending of the knees
With age, a difficult task
Pains are awaken

Coupled with my health
If I live four scores and ten
Blessings will be seen

Wobbling and stumbling

Turning The Pages   James Smith

Harder getting around towns
Thankful and alive
Drugs are companions
Making life more bearable
As the years add up

What I use to be
The heroics of my youth
Memories retain

Many miles behind me
The future nearer than far
Last days getting close

Wisdom in my reigns
Looking back at brighter days
Before passing on

The body falters
When the keepers of the house
Yield before old age

A leader of men
Child to man to child again
Others will lead me

Youths should serve the Lord
Burdens of arthritis
Summon the aged

As age continues
Memory will leave its nest
Erasing knowledge

Turning The Pages   James Smith

Wisdom blooms brighter
Maturity grows with years
Knowledge increases

Fear of heights and depths
The child I once was returns
In need of guidance

Unable to rise
Looking up at the ceiling
Movement restricted

Hearing is failing
Sight and speech both getting blur
Shaking and trembling

A bare footed boy
When years added upon him
The bed confined him

What birth gave, youth took
Adulthood embraced it
But death will take it

Past evils come back
Restitution seeks revenge
Escape is futile

The aged recalls
The attributes of their youth
What was is no more

Turning The Pages   James Smith

When manhood ceases,
The will to perform rises
Only in the mind

As a man ages,
The crown of knowledge grows bare
Wisdom gets foolish

Naked and hungry
From us they enter this life
Criminals and saints

Summary

Sin was the cause and is still the cause of mankind' down fall. Modern man keeps following the steps of formal man. He seems bent on testing God wrath. Man is not heeding the example of what happened to those that broke God law during the Old Testament ere. Sin is on the rise and getting worse and worse each day. Fast living and material wealth appear to be more important even to church going people than seeking to learn and follow God word. The scriptures are been fulfilled before our eyes each and every day but it seem to have no effect on the so-called Christian community. If the Christian community is not moved by the evils that are going on around them, how do they expect the unsaved to act?

Manipulation, the same tactic the devil used in deceiving humankind from the beginning, is still very much at work today creating the same affect. Witchcraft and black magic were sources of manipulation in and prior to the Middle Ages but today Manipulators only need words. Once people become blinded by their sale pitch; they become vulnerable to manipulation week after week, year after year, without even realizing the influence these people hold over their lives. The late Jim Jones and the various cult leaders of the past and present are typical examples of Manipulators using words to deceive masses of people. However, Manipulators are not just confined to the leaders of the past and cult leaders there are many of them operating in government offices, and churches

today. These men and women are not concerned about
God or the people they're pretending to serve; their main
concern is filling the financial and lustful desires of their
heart.

**Second Timothy two fifteen says, study to show
thyself approved unto God, a workman that needeth not
to be ashamed rightly dividing the word of truth.** Take a
little time to read and study the bible for yourself; pray
and meditate on the word daily; seek the guidance of the
Holy Spirit in your life. The spirit, which is the comforter,
that Jesus promised would be sent from the Father, will
guide you in the things and ways you should go. To
receive the gift of the Holy Spirit, you must first
acknowledge your sin, repent, believe in Jesus Christ, be
baptized, and become reborn again in order for God to
hear and acknowledge your prayer or crown you with the
gift of the Holy Spirit. Once you've accepted Christ as your
Savior and he has chosen you, you can begin on the road
to truth. No longer will you have to wonder whether
you're saved or not; you'll understand what baptism does
for you; embrace the ordeals of the communion table and
realize how love plays a part in all that the Christian man
and woman do and says.

You'll seek not the riches of this world which you
would someday lose but the riches that God have to offer
through the gift of the Holy Spirit which we never lose as
long as we remain faithful. The life we live have a greater
bearing on people than the words we speak. **A mind may
be a terrible thing to waste but a soul is a greater thing to
lose.** We place great emphasis on people getting the
knowledge the world has to offer but give little
consideration to knowledge that can save a sin sick soul

from everlasting damnation. Remember what God says in the book of Hosea. "My people are destroyed for lack of knowledge Hosea 4:6a." The people of Hosea' ere was being destroyed because of their lack of knowledge. As it was available to Israel, knowledge is available today and people are still being destroyed for their lack of it.

In Hosea ere, we don't really know how available knowledge was but we know for sure how available it is today. Nearly, if not every family, in America has the word of God at their finger tip. Whether it's in the form of a bible, record, C D, tape, Ipad, or tablet, if not owned, they're available for our use. If a table filled with all sorts of food was place before a starving man and he died because he refused to eat, it would be his own false. Mankind is faced with that same dilemma today. The truth to eternal life is within our grabs; all that any man or woman has to do is accept it, believe it, and the one who offers forgiveness, and salvation **(eternal life)** can be theirs. But if one refuses to accept and believe in the word, which is Jesus Christ, according to St. John 1:1, he is condemned already because he hath not believed in the name of the only begotten Son of God, St. John3:18.

Death was once confined mostly to old age but in this day and time it seems young people are dying and being killed by one another as rapid as the aged are dying of natural deaths. The scripture speaks of our days being three scores and ten **(70 years)** and if by reason of strength they be four score years, **(80 years)** they'll be filled with labor and sorrow **(a lot of hard work and disappointments)** These words were written by David in Psalm 90:10 and supported by Job 14:1 which says, "man that is born of a woman is of few days, and full of troubles". Just as the fifth commandment is based upon children obedient to their parents and God, Adults life span is based upon their obedient to God and one another. Obedient and respect are becoming a thing of the past. Few children respect their parents, teachers, the elderly, or God; few adults, including church going people, respect God or one another today. There's a wrath being poured upon the earth today like nothing we've seen before. Cities and lives are being destroyed by floods, earth quakes, mud slides, tornados, twisters, fires, terrorist bombs, and all sorts of outrageous crimes. In the midst of all these, men refuse to repent or pray. God' blessings upon ancient Israel depended upon their being faithful to God and his commandments. Keep in mind that God is the same yesterday, and today, and ever more and that he requires the same of us today as he required of those in the past. The righteous can change the things that are going on in our societies today.

We know that God is true to his promises. In 2 chronicles 7:12-14, we see the answer God gives Solomon in answer to his prayer after finishing the building of the house of God. God says in the thirteenth verse "if I shut up heaven that there be no rain, or if I command the locusts to devour the land, or if I send pestilence among my people; if my people, which are called by my name, shall humble themselves, and pray, and seek my face, and turn from their wicked ways; then will I hear from heaven, and will forgive their sin, and will heal the land." Here God tells Solomon, the leader of his people, that if disasters are sent upon the land and the people that are called by his name humble themselves and pray, and seek to bring him into their lives by turning from their wicked ways then he **(God),** would and still will for us today heal the land and forgive our sins. Sin is the cause of God wrath being sent upon our land and if we want God to heal it by removing the evils that are pledging us, then, not mankind in general, God' people, Christian people, must humble themselves and pray in unity but the prayer must be sincere and the people must repent and turn back to God. Many church leaders quote this scripture but they do nothing toward leading their congregation to humble themselves in prayer and repentance to fulfill the scripture. Man cannot solve our problems yet we refuse to call on the one that can. If we're too proud to ask, we only hurt ourselves. Ministers seem to be reluctant to get together concerning spiritual matters. A house divided against its self cannot stand. These are words of our Lord and Savior, Jesus Christ. By the annoying of God laws by our states and federal governments, it is causing chaos among the world. By accepting and supporting ungodly people and things in the church, it has and continues to cause division, confusion, doubts, and mistrust among church people.

The first world' destruction was because of mankind' continued pursuit of evil. While mankind continues in his evil ways today, God is looking on with an unpleased heart. In the books of St. Matthew chapter 24: 6-8, and St. Mark chapter 13:7-8, Jesus gives us a list of things to look for that will announce the beginning of sorrows for mankind sins. We see those things going on today but mankind seems more pleased than sorrow. Be aware, a day of reckoning awakes, God is not mocked.

About The Author

The author is a poet, play writer, Sunday school teacher, religious writer, bible puzzle maker, and hobbyist. He truly enjoys studying and discussing the bible. In his free time, he devotes himself to his diver hobbies. This book completes his second religious book and eleventh book over all. The author also has a deep concern for righteousness. He is involved in various ways of introducing people to the ways and word of God. Seeing the decline in church attendance, this author tries to serve in word and example striving to be a help to as many people as possible in the allotted time God has given him.